simple·ology

simple·ology

The Simple Science of
Getting What You Want

MARK JOYNER

John Wiley & Sons, Inc.

Published by John Wiley & Sons, Inc., Hoboken, New Jersey.
Published simultaneously in Canada.

Wiley Bicentennial Logo: Richard J. Pacifico

For general information on our other products and services please contact our Customer Care Department within the United States at (800) 762-2974, outside the United States at (317) 572-3993 or fax (317) 572-4002.

Wiley also publishes its books in a variety of electronic formats. Some content that appears in print may not be available in electronic books. For more information about Wiley products, visit our web site at www.wiley.com.

Library of Congress Cataloging-in-Publication Data:

Joyner, Mark, 1968–
  Simpleology : the simple science of getting what you want / Mark Joyner.
    p.   cm.
  ISBN 978-0-470-09522-5 (cloth : alk. paper)
1. Self-actualization (Psychology) 2. Success. 3. Success in business. I. Title.
  BF637.S4J69 2007
  158—dc22

                                                            2006033464

Printed in the United States of America.

10 9 8 7 6 5 4 3 2 1

Contents

Before You Get Started

Let's face it: books are old school.

I love to hold a book in my hands. I love the way it looks on my shelf. But if I really want to master something, I need to engage myself in its *application*.

Reading is one thing. Understanding is another. And proper application is a whole 'nother thing entirely.

If you want to sound knowledgeable at dinner parties, stopping at the level of understanding is okay.

If, however, you want to achieve something unusual (for example obscene sit-on-your-butt-for-the-rest-of-your-life wealth, Tiger Woods greatness, Mick Jagger rock stardom, Donald Trump luxury), proper application is where it's at.

But don't despair!

The book you hold in your hands comes packed with a few hidden surprises to take you there (the best of which you'll discover by the time you finish reading the last pages of this book, but don't peek; it will be much better that way).

simple•ology: The Simple Science of Getting What You Want is merely the companion to a multimedia learning experience and some life-changing software—all of which you can access for free.

These tools will not only help you master the information found herein, but also *apply* it to your daily life.

How can that be?

Check it out.

Before you get started, please enter this URL in your web browser:

http://www.FreeWebCockpit.com

It will take just a few seconds to set up your free *simple•*ology account and you'll have instant free access to the full *simple•*ology 101 multimedia companion course and WebCockpit software.

This is essential! We've made all of this available to you completely free of charge, so please do this now before you begin reading the book.

Then you can use it to supplement your learning; curled up in bed, in a cafe, on the bus, or wherever you want.

Enjoy the free software and multimedia experience!

Mark Joyner

March 2007

Introduction:
Getting What We Want

I have no idea what you want.

I have no business telling you what to want.

My job is to help you get it—whatever it is.

*simple•*ology, as a system of seeing the world and *acting* in the world for your desired effects, will do just that. Not only will you get what you want, but you'll get it faster and with the least possible effort.

Notice I said "least possible effort"—not "easy."

If you want a bogus rah-rah self-help manual that blows a song of sunshine up your back door, then you've got the wrong book.

If you want a book that teaches you "magical thinking"— one that teaches you how to hope, pray, and meditate on what you want and "let the universe do the work for you" while you sit on your butt high on ganja and dogma, again, you've got the wrong book.

If, however, you want to get things "for real," then you're in the right place.

The good news is, while you're not going to snap your fingers and watch a new house fall from the sky, getting the things you want is probably much easier than you think.

More about that shortly.

So What Do You Want?

Maybe you want a great big dream house just high enough on the hill overlooking the beach for people to look at in envy.

Maybe you want a pimped-out car that will make people turn their heads as you drive by.

Maybe you want a superhot lover who thinks you're a slice of fried heaven.

Well, right now those things are *thoughts* inside your mind.

Is it possible to turn those thoughts into reality?

Actually it is. In fact, everything ever made by a person started out as a thought inside someone's head.

Before Bill Gates became the richest man in the world, there was a time when he was a flat broke student sitting in a chair somewhere and he had a thought

An idea

A vision

A notion

I want to start a software company.

Somehow, this thought became a reality.

That's amazingly cool, really, when you think about it.

A thought in the head of *someone just like you* turned into a fantastic reality.

And this kind of thought-to-reality transformation is far from uncommon.

From the hit songs on your MP3 player, to the skyscrapers on the San Francisco skyline, to the hottest club in Tokyo, to the funky clothes on your back: All of these things began as a thought in someone's mind, and their reality can be plainly observed by you right now.

As you read this book, perhaps some of the thoughts in your head could become reality, too.

Will they?

Let's find out.

There are millions of other people who, like Bill Gates, have had the notion to start a software company. What happened to them?

Well . . .

Some of them never started any software company at all.

Some of them started small software companies that were not very successful.

Some of them are doing something else and every day when they stare down that *gulf-between-their-dream-and-what-they-want* it fills them with sadness.

Some of them started companies, did millions of dollars in sales, and then ended up selling the companies off (the guy writing these words did that).

Some of them thought they had started a software company, but hadn't, and are living in asylums.

What's the difference?

Why did the notion of one person become one reality and the notions of others become another? And why did the notions of some not become reality at all?

This book shows you, quite clearly and *simply*, how this came to be so—and then shows you plainly and clearly how to bridge your own gap between your dreams and reality.

In the simplest sense, the answer is found in The First Law of *simple•*ology: The Law of Straight Lines. *That is, "the shortest path between any two points is a straight line."*

We all instinctively know this to be true, but our actions are usually radically curvy lines, or straight lines in the wrong direction.

By focusing exclusively on *the simple actions that work* to achieve your desired results, you get them in the fastest possible way with the least possible effort.

That's *simple•*ology.

You could go to Book IV right now and begin learning these practical ideas and applying them for immediate benefit. In fact, in your *simple•*ology 101 multimedia companion course, that is our starting point. We teach you the practical side of *simple•*ology and give you software to actually implement it in your daily life.

We start you there so you can begin to see immediate and astonishingly positive changes in your life *right now*.

But in the context of a print book, we can dig a little deeper into *why* people fall off the straight line path.

To do this, we have to take a trip together. It will be like watching a movie. But I have to warn you: This isn't a feel-good movie or a fantasy.

At times it will feel like a dime store pulp detective novel.

Sometimes it will feel like a psychological thriller.

Other times it will feel like screwball shock comedy.

And at other times it will feel like a horror film.

But I can assure you, you'll like the ending.

Read—err . . . *watch* on.

Book I:
The Asylum

Why you're stuck where you are now.

You are here.

Book II:
The Invisible Walls

Your defective mental hardware and other programming anomalies that prevent you from getting what you want.

Offensive weapons used against you to keep you there.

Book III:
Disposable Reality

A new Operating System for the brain.

Defensive weapons to break your way out.

Book IV:
*simple•*ology

The Simple Science of Getting What You Want

The Programming Language for writing programs that turn dreams into reality.

How to get to where you want to be.

The Asylum

Insanity

Sometimes, to get the things we want, we do strange things.

Sometimes they work.

Sometimes they don't.

And that's okay! If nobody tried anything new, we'd be stuck with the "same old things" and that would make life boring.

Some of the crazy things we try even end up changing the world.

Louis Pasteur, the man who first had the notion that certain germs in our body are associated with illness, was referred to by his peers as a "crackpot." Anyone who catches a used-

to-be-life-threatening disease today and cures it with an antibiotic might call him something else: a "genius."

See, the problem isn't trying unusual things. The problem is doing things that don't serve our aims, but erroneously thinking they do.

Sometimes this takes the form of:

> *Insanity: doing the same thing over and over again and expecting different results.*
>
> —Albert Einstein

Einstein was halfway there. This is but one of many flavors of craziness we may experience on a daily basis.

Misunderstanding the world around us drives us crazy.

Other people manipulating us and our not understanding *how*, drives us crazy, too.

From time to time, we're all a little bit crazy, and that's okay, really.

Inevitable even.

It's just that the results we get from crazy are anything but what we *want* in life.

Insanity?

A clinical psychologist might have a few issues with Einstein's definition. In fact, there is a whole source book (DSM IV) that outlines and categorizes different forms of mental illness.

This kind of knowledge, outside of a clinical setting, may not be very useful.

Therefore, we'll look at common everyday garden variety insanity and some practical ways of dealing with it.

Don't think it applies to you? Read on: I guarantee you'll be surprised.

In one sense, anything that we allow to pull us off the path to *getting what we want* is a type of insanity.

That definition works well for our context.

In order to get what you want, you have to step outside of crazy and step into . . .

Science

The opposite of insanity is science.

Science isn't really about lab coats and beakers; it's about a *useful* way of looking at the world.

Science

Try it.
Pay attention.
If it works—great!
Now you know a little something.
If not, you can try something else.
Take notes.

Insanity

Try it.
Don't pay attention.
If it doesn't work—keep doing it over and over again anyway.
(Notes not recommended.)

There's a bit more you need to understand about science that we cover later, but you get the idea.

Now, you could probably read these two chapters, close this book, and walk away with one of the most important concepts the world has to offer.

Truly.

. . . but wait.

Understanding the nature of science is powerful. Maybe the most powerful thing.

But there is something else science gives us: *knowledge*.

Scientists have come and gone through the ages, but they have left for you (at least the good ones have) a record of what works and what doesn't.

Isn't that handy?

Rather than take random stabs in the dark at life, we can open up a book and say, "Hey, this guy tried this and he says it worked. Let me try it and see for myself."

Note that you said, "Let *me* try it and see for myself."

Warning: Just because it worked for someone else, doesn't mean it will work for you.

Some of the knowledge you gain will work. Some of it won't. But it's sure great that it's there. Even better is your ability to find out *for yourself* if it's true.

This all seems quite simple, and it is!

What Do You Mean *Scientist?*

Just because someone is a scientist (in the university and lab coat sense) doesn't mean that they always think and act like a scientist.

Scientists are human beings just like you and have the same failings.

Some are better than others. Some can make genius leaps forward one day and colossal blunders the next.

So, let's not confuse these things. I'm not talking about donning a lab coat. I'm talking about *thinking* and *acting* like a scientist in the *spirit* of scientific exploration.

What does that mean? Read on.

If it's so simple, then how come people are still doing crazy things?

Why is it that when they want the Ferrari they engage in ineffectual behavior that will give them anything but?

Well, for starters, you live in an asylum and that asylum has invisible walls.

11

Chapter 2: Science

The Invisible Walls Around the Asylum

Even those of us who understand science intellectually, still keep *doing* crazy things.

Why is that?

Consider this story.

As I write this book, I live in Auckland, New Zealand. Every day I walk to my secret boutique office space from my townhouse hidden in the inner city.

Along one of the varying routes I take in the morning (varying your route every day is good for the brain), I pass a ground floor office space with wide open windows.

If you were to walk past it, you'd see two main sections.

In the first you'd see a very bare-looking room with three desks. At each desk you'd see people who are clearly "the workers."

When they're not farting around and joking with each other, they are playing solitaire on their computers, or staring at their screens without really doing anything effectual—occasionally looking around perhaps to check if the guy in the next room is coming.

The guy in the next room is a very tired, overweight, middle-aged guy—quite clearly "the boss."

Minus the farting around he's doing pretty much the same as the rest of his team: not much.

The only difference is the scowl on his face.

Book I: The Asylum

You can tell that the cash flow is probably pretty thin and he doesn't have the first idea of what to do about that.

He's not *doing* anything, but gosh darnit, he means it.

He probably learned somewhere along the way that his staff will walk all over him unless he is strict and stern—hence, the scowl.

But strict and stern about what?

This morning as I walked by, there was a difference. In the first room, everything was as it normally was.

In the second room the "boss man" had buried his face in his hands and his shoulders were in a slump.

I wonder how many more days of this are left.

And I wonder why this has carried on for so long.

The picture I've just painted is probably not so uncommon at all.

It probably wouldn't take much research to prove that the average worker gets only about 30 minutes to 1 hour of actual work done every day.

If you brought up this fact to the average office worker, you'd probably get a nervous laugh and a nod of agreement.

Then they'd go back to the same old ineffective routine.

And then the boss man might bring in some experts.

"The problem is improper training and improper motivation."

Chapter 3: The Invisible Walls Around the Asylum

Eureka!

So, we bring in the experts.

They teach us their magic tricks.

And then what?

Well, a few days of increased productivity may follow, but then inevitably . . .

It's back to the same old routine.

But we expected that, didn't we?

See, we all know this is going on but aren't doing anything about it.

16

If you were to ask the office worker why this was so, you'd probably get a universal "Uhhh I dunno . . . maybe . . ." followed by a (likely to be insightful) stab in the dark about the reasons.

And that's about as far as the average person goes in attempting to slap some paint on these Invisible Walls.

What forces are at play here?

Here's another story that might provide some clues.

Let's take a hypothetical guy named Dave.

Is Dave a *real* guy?

You'll know by the time you finish reading this book (I mean watching this movie).

The other night Dave was at the local pub and as usual the pub rats were on one of "the three topics you can't discuss at the dinner table":

Religion

Politics

Sex

This time it was politics. The topic: whether a flat sales tax and abolition of the income tax would be good for the country.

Dave likes the flat tax. It makes good sense to him. In fact, he even knows of a really smart university professor, Dr. Fancypants, who agrees with him.

17

DAVE

Well, if you agree with Dr. Fancypants, the flat tax will make our economy boom. He says that the flat tax was tested way back in 1431 in Middleanowheria and that the economy flourished for 30 years until Count Itsallmine reinstated the income tax.

PUB RAT #1

Is that so?

DAVE

Yeah, it sure is. And a lot of people now are wondering why we never did it.

PUB RAT #2

Hey, isn't Dr. Fancypants the guy who was caught at a Klan rally?

(All laugh.)

And the topic of a flat tax was never brought up again. At least not without the Dr. Fancypants jokes.

For some reason, Dave felt odd every time he thought of Dr. Fancypants from that point forward.

The truth of the matter is Dr. Fancypants was in fact a member of the Ku Klux Klan. Simultaneously, he was one of the best economic thinkers in history.

But his brilliance no longer mattered. All anyone remembers after the media smear campaign (funded, of course, by those who oppose his flat tax plan) is "Fancypants—KKK."

Dave knew in that moment that something wasn't quite right, but he couldn't put his finger on it.

It made him slightly angry even.

Instead of articulating this discomfort or trying to figure out why he felt it, he just clammed up and never spoke of Fancypants again.

What Dave didn't know was that Pub Rat #2 used a very common "logical fallacy" known as:

Argumentum ad hominem   It's Latin for "arguing against the man."

Instead of addressing the argument itself, the perpetrator of this fallacy attacks you or the people behind your information.

This is a "fallacy" because it's altogether possible that Dr. Fancypants is both a member of the KKK *and* right about the flat tax at the same time.

But that's not how we think.

This particular tool is but one of many linguistic artifacts that bind our minds.

While *argumentum ad hominem* is invalid, it *does* have an effect on the listener.

It puts a little frame around the information, and frames affect perception.

Words have other ways of binding us as well.

Sometimes when we do crazy things, we cook up language that will lock us into that pattern.

19

Chapter 3: The Invisible Walls Around the Asylum

Dave was back at the bar again.

Pub Rat #1 had just picked up a new hobby: recreational inhalants.

This is a surprisingly common form of drug abuse in which one inhales the fumes of adhesives (glue), solvents, aerosols, or other common industrial or household chemicals.

One inhales the fumes, and as the chemicals dissolve brain cell membranes, you experience a cheap high.

You read that right: "dissolve brain cell membranes."

PUB RAT #1

Dude, you have to try it.

DAVE

Really? What's it like?

PUB RAT #1

Well, at first you feel like you're choking. Then you feel like you're really really, high. It's better than sex.

DAVE

I dunno, man. It sounds pretty dangerous.

PUB RAT #1

Ah, don't be a wuss! You only live once, man!

Well, that may be true; as far as anyone knows for sure, we may only live once. At least, there doesn't seem to be any universally agreed upon evidence to the contrary.

And, in fact, sometimes people don't take risks because they are indeed wusses.

Hmm . . . tempting!

In that moment, Dave was considering giving this glue sniffing business a shot. I mean, Pub Rat #1 did have some good points.

What could be wrong with it?

What Dave wasn't thinking about in that moment was that while it may be that we only live once, sniffing industrial chemicals could bring that only-happens-once deal to a swifter close.

(For your "don't try this at home" file: This practice causes accidental deaths every year.)

Chapter 3: The Invisible Walls Around the Asylum

More importantly for us, Dave was stuck between two options:

1. Being a wuss and failing to enjoy life.
2. Sniffing some oven cleaner.

This is what most will call a catch-22 (from the great novel of the same name), a dilemma, or a no-win situation.

More formally it is referred to as a:

Double Bind (Definition #1)

A formal definition from the great anthropologist and linguist Gregory Bateson: *An unresolvable dilemma whereby two conflicting, or equally unsavory, options are presented by an authority figure to an unwitting victim.* This can cause severe distress or even psychosis. "Damned if you *do*, damned if you *don't*."

Bateson coined the phrase as a theory of schizophrenia. His full definition is more complex, but you get the idea.

Many normal people, not just those on the path to schizophrenia, are affected by double binds every day. Probably most frequently:

Double Bind (Definition #2)

A more common and less formal definition as used by pop persuasion experts: *The proposition of two unsavory options—one painted in a favorable light in order to influence behavior.* ("What are you? A wuss? Come on, just sniff the glue.")

22

In both cases, it's the inability of the victim to see through the double bind that causes problems.

What do I mean by that?

Back to Dave and the oven cleaner.

In that moment Dave failed to realize that there were, in fact, other options. The double bind itself is an illusion, but the victim does not realize it.

When the mind treats it as real the effects can be catastrophic.

It's quite common really.

But the solution . . .

PUB RAT #1
Choose A or B! Which is it gonna be?

DAVE
Actually, I'll choose *C*. Or *D*. Or something else altogether. See ya, loser.

. . . is not.

In fact, many of the great works of literature are about people who live in the imaginary prison a double bind creates.

A great example of that is *Zen and the Art of Motorcycle Maintenance* (Pirsig 1974). This very long but fascinating book is a chronicle of one extremely intelligent man's struggle with a rather lofty double bind.

23

Chapter 3: The Invisible Walls Around the Asylum

I won't spoil the ending, but you already have a hint.

Here's another: *mu*. (Google it.)

Anyway, it just goes to show that sanity has little to do with how intelligent you are.

It has much more to do with having a *useful* understanding of the world.

Those are two of the many forms in which these Invisible Walls manifest themselves. You'll notice they are both related to language.

Words are even more powerful than you may think. In 1977 a preacher named Jim Jones cooked up some words that persuaded 1,000 people to leave their homes in the United

The Intelligence Trap

Edward De Bono went as far as to say that intelligence itself could even trap you and prevent you from solving problems.

See, one form of intelligence is the inherent ability to argue your point. According to De Bono, the smarter you are, the better you are at verbal justification, so this will in fact prevent you from learning and problem solving. It binds you to an unhealthy way of living—you just talk yourself into it.

States and set up a religious community in "Jonestown," Guiana.

In 1978 he cooked up some other words that persuaded 914 of them to end their lives by drinking grape flavored Kool-Aid laced with cyanide.

Their double bind: Face the evils of the outside world or drink this Kool-Aid and find salvation.

Sign me up!

Language has also been used to start wars, riots, and all sorts of mayhem all throughout history.

Chapter 3: The Invisible Walls Around the Asylum

But language isn't all bad. The great clinical hypnotist Milton H. Erickson used linguistic tricks (even double binds) in a therapeutic setting to trick people into happiness and healthier behavior.

Now, you may think that you've got this Invisible Wall thing licked, but hold your horses.

Language isn't the only thing that binds us, and the Invisible Walls aren't the only problem.

Your Escape Route

As you gain greater awareness of the various Invisible Walls, their hold on you lessens more and more over time.

It's quite liberating!

By the time you finish Book II, you'll know more about them than anyone else on your block.

But first there are two other things you need:

1. A meaningful way to think about the information you receive.

2. A navigation system to guide you on the path between your dreams and reality.

On the surface, the idea of "Try it. If it works—great! If it doesn't, try something else," makes perfect sense. But it's not that simple.

Remember Dave?

Well, Dave went to a workshop last week to learn some pickup tactics to make him more popular with the ladies.

One of them was the My Indian Name pickup line (don't try this at home; I'm really just making this up).

DAVE

Hi, I'm Dave, but my Indian name is *Makes Love All Night Like a Stallion and Cooks You Breakfast.*

CANDY

You're funny. Let's get out of here, Mr. whatever-your-name-is.

Score!

So Dave, scientist that he was, thought he had it all figured out. He tried it. It worked. Now all he had to do was the same thing again.

Right?

The next night . . .

DAVE

Hi, I'm Dave, but my Indian name is *Makes Love All Night Like a Stallion and Cooks You Breakfast.*

RUNNING BEAR

Oh, yeah? Well, my name is Running Bear. I really *am* Indian. Your ancestors killed my ancestors. Die, white man!

(Running Bear scalps Dave. Dave exits.)

What went wrong?

Night after night, like a good little scientist, Dave tried new pickup lines (starting this time with one that wasn't a racial slur) and over time he developed a little routine that was working for him relatively consistently.

Then one day, all of a sudden, it stopped working.

Dave couldn't figure it out.

What he didn't realize was that on the day it stopped working, he had changed deodorant brands. The new brand had a chemical that was actually proven to make female mammals perceive a threat to their babies.

The advertising hadn't mentioned this. (And some day in the future someone will discover a memo that shows that the CEO of the company knew full well that his deodorant was female-repellant. Ironically, they named it "Superstud.")

Anyway, none of this helped Dave.

A better understanding of the world would have helped, though (as would a change in his unhealthy obsession with getting laid).

That's what Book III is all about. It gives you some extremely powerful tools for improving the accuracy with which you evaluate the information around you.

With it, you'll know how to evaluate that information in a healthy way.

This makes you a great observer, but you want to be a *doer*, right?

This is, after all, a book about The Simple Science of Getting What You Want.

Book IV gives you a useful system for *acting* in the world that will greatly speed up the rate at which you get the things you want—cutting through all the nonsense and insanity that doesn't work right to what does.

But you're not ready for that yet.

First, we must get a deeper understanding of why you're *not* getting what you want now.

We must understand why our actions benefit others more than they benefit ourselves.

We must take a deeper look at . . .

Book I:
The Asylum

Why you're stuck where you are now.

Book II:
The Invisible Walls

Your defective mental hardware and other programming anomalies that prevent you from getting what you want.

Offensive weapons used against you to keep you there.

You are here.

Book III:
Disposable Reality

A new Operating System for the brain.

Defensive weapons to break your way out.

Book IV:
simple•ology
The Simple Science of Getting What You Want

The Programming Language for writing programs that turn dreams into reality.

How to get to where you want to be.

The Invisible Walls

Introduction

What follows is by no means a complete treatment of this topic, but it will certainly begin to open up some doors in your mind.

I have to warn you, though. Many people when first exposed to these ideas begin to struggle. It's not that the ideas are particularly hard to grasp (they're not). The trouble is that those exposed to them will challenge things they hold dear.

Letting go of them is easier said than done.

However, as you'll find as you read along, this process is not only rewarding but may even be necessary for your mental well-being.

After this, you should remain a lifelong student of these topics so that you get greater and greater control of your own mind and therefore your life.

We're a long way from having complete understanding of the human mind despite what some of the multi-flavored-snake-oil peddling charlatans of the world will have you believe.

But we do have a great number of clues. Some of the best of them follow.

Your Model of the World

There's a movie playing in your head right now.

> It is loosely related to the real world, but it's not the real world.
>
> Some of it is based on observed fact.
>
> More of it is based on good hunches.
>
> And even more is based on wild imagination.

But there is one thing it's not—even though you use this name for it: reality.

We know very little about the human brain right now, but we do know this:

> *What we actually see on the outside isn't the outside world at all.*

You think that what you're looking at "is what it is," but what you're actually "seeing" is a *simulation* of what "is" coming in through your senses.

Huh?

To help you understand: Every now and then a crazy guy everyone calls The Fool walks into Dave's favorite pub. He orders a pint, sits down, and out of the blue will ask the pub patrons really random questions. Like . . .

THE FOOL

Dave, my boy, describe to me the process of seeing.

DAVE

Umm . . . *seeing?* You mean like with my eyes?

THE FOOL

That's a start.

DAVE

Well, hmm . . . I guess it must be like radar, right? I mean, we must shoot out some wave or something that bounces off the things we look at and then when it comes back, we see it.

THE FOOL

Not a bad theory, but most scientists believe it's the other way around.

DAVE

You mean that things bounce radar off us?

THE FOOL

Not things. Light. Start with the light source.

36

Book II: The Invisible Walls

DAVE

Ah . . . right. So light bounces off an object and then puts the image into our brain?

THE FOOL

You're half right. The light doesn't put the image into our brain. Light is only a carrier of information. Our eyes actually receive the information and send it to our brain. Our brain then constructs an interpretation of that data. It's like a replica of the data living inside your mind.

DAVE

So, we're not really seeing what's there?

THE FOOL

Nope. It's a replica. And this replica can actually be distorted in many ways and often is.

DAVE

Trippy.

THE FOOL

It gets trippier. Do you have a fish?

DAVE

No, fish are for sissies.

THE FOOL

Dave, I know you have a fish. Anyway, your fish can actually see things you can't see.

DAVE

Shut up.

THE FOOL

Seriously. Some fish can actually see in *infrared*.

37

Chapter 1: Your Model of the World

DAVE

You mean like night vision goggles?

THE FOOL

I mean exactly like that, but hold on. Do you actually know what infrared is?

DAVE

Actually, no.

THE FOOL

Well, you're probably familiar with the colors of the rainbow. There's a useful mnemonic for remembering them: ROYGBIV—red orange yellow green blue indigo violet.

DAVE

You *are* a sissy.

THE FOOL

Shut up. Anyway, ROYGBIV is only a small section of what they call the *electromagnetic spectrum*. If red were on the right and you continued moving along, the next thing you'd have is infrared. Further along you'd have *microwaves*. If you carried on to the end, you'd have *radiowaves* and then *long waves*. On the opposite end you'd have *X-rays* and *gamma rays*. What you *see* is only a tiny fraction of that, and your fish can see more of it than you.

DAVE

Damn.

THE FOOL

Exactly.

DAVE

Holy . . . Hey, that's why X-rays work, isn't it? We're seeing in X-rays?

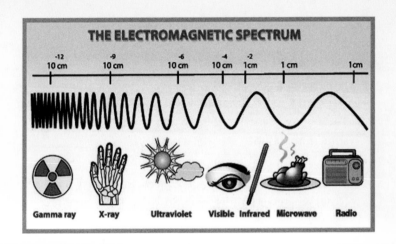

THE FOOL

Not bad, but not exactly. When you go to the doctor and *see* an X-ray of your body, you're not seeing *in* X-rays yourself, but you're seeing an interpretation of what the X-ray can see. It has to be translated into a form that we can see ourselves.

DAVE

Hey, what if we could see in microwaves?

THE FOOL

Now you're thinking. It's a good question—what if?

So, our visual replica of the world is actually only a tiny fraction of a much larger reality.

To make matters worse, the actual process of seeing itself may in fact change the object that is being seen.

39

This has to do with a phenomenon known as the "observer effect."

This phrase has a few varied meanings and interpretations, but the easiest way to look at it is this:

> To observe something, in any way, you have to bounce something off it.
>
> As we learned from The Fool, the act of seeing starts with light bouncing off the object and into your eyes. Now, whatever light is, we know that it has an effect on objects it touches.
>
> Therefore, what you *see* has been changed in some way before it even hits your eyes.

Does this hold true for *every* way of observing?

As far as we know now it does.

Take an electron microscope: How does it work? By bombarding the object with, well, electrons.

Electrons are *matter* and this act changes, in ways about which we can never be certain, the object being observed.

A fascinating corollary of this is found in experimental science. It has been found that the presence, and expectation, of an observer can in fact affect the outcome of it. So much for "seeing is believing," huh?

And vision is only part of the picture.

Our model of the world is comprised not only of what we see, but also of what we hear, feel, and think.

Sadly, and perhaps thankfully, this model will always, by definition, be incomplete.

There are certain limitations hardwired into our brains that make it so.

First, it's impossible for us to know everything. It shouldn't take much evidence to prove this to you. But try this if you're not sure:

> Pull out a map of the world, close your eyes, and point your finger at a random spot.
>
> Now ask yourself: Do you know what language is spoken there? Do you know what religious beliefs are common there? Do you know what form of government they practice? Do you know what street the capital building is on?

I think you get the point. It's impossible for us to know everything.

Even more, it's impossible for us to keep more than a tiny fraction of what we do know in our minds at the same time.

The Magic Number 7

Princeton University cognitive psychologist George Miller wrote a paper in 1956 titled "The Magical Number Seven, Plus or Minus Two: Some Limits on Our Capacity for Processing Information." In it, he observed that the human mind can hold only between five and nine units of information consciously at a time.

You probably have quite a bit of knowledge tucked away in your mind, but you can consciously think about only a tiny fraction of it at a time.

Chapter 1: Your Model of the World

Now, for the icing on the cake . . .

In addition to all of the hard-wired limitations built in to our brains, our model of the world . . .

> *That is: what we believe to be true, or that picture in our mind of what comprises "the real world," or our version of "Truth . . ."*

. . . is based not only on the limited "hard" information of our senses, but also our own abstract beliefs, ideas, theories, and imaginings.

Sometimes these things have absolutely no basis in observable reality at all, but we act as if they do.

Some may say this sometimes antagonistic interaction of our fanciful view of reality and contrary information is the primary illness of man.

We'll talk more about that later. For now, here is a useful model I've created to help you put all this together.

Imagine for a moment that your brain functions in many ways just like a computer. We'll call this . . .

The Brain as Personal Computer Model

- What you know, your stored information, is like the hard drive.
- What you can hold in your mind right now and process at this moment, is like the RAM.
- The central processing unit (CPU) in a computer has a built-in ability to process information and also has a

hardwired set of rules for doing so. Any changes in a computer's program have to be written in ways that pay respect to this. The same holds when you are programming your own mind.

- The models of the world that you create are like the Operating System (OS).
- The things that you do are like the programs you run on top of the OS.

Let's look at the chart below.

We still have much to learn about the mind, but this model can provide some clues.

We don't know exactly how information (our memories and thoughts) are stored inside our "hard drives." We don't even know how much information can be stored there.

Computer Hardware	Brain Hardware
CPU	Your mental processing power and hardwired rules for processing.
RAM	The amount of info you can process at once.
Hard Drive	Your stored information, stored thoughts, stored memories, stored experiences.
Operating System	Your model of the world.
Programs	How you function in the world to obtain various ends.

What we do know is that all of the information is *networked* in constantly evolving patterns. We believe that information is stored in neurons and that new connections between neurons are being made all the time.

For example, when looking at the chart on the preceding page, it's likely that you made some brand new (and very useful) connection between two ideas that, up to this point, were not connected.

So we know that the brain stores raw information like a hard drive, but on top of that raw data is a web of connections that help us organize it.

Yet ultimately, we still know relatively little about the way this works. We're making new discoveries every day, and we are regularly surprised.

We also know very little of the mechanisms of consciousness, but we do have a few clues like The Magic Number 7.

The interaction, and occasional dysfunction, of your hard drive and RAM can be observed by the following phenomenon.

Have you ever had an argument with someone and in the middle of it they say, "Yes, but if you look at what Dr. Respectmybrain said about that . . ."?

Oh. Damn. That *is* a good point.

That particular connection wasn't present (or strong enough) in your mind, so you wern't aware of that fact in the moment.

There's a lot more to it, but you get the idea. The rest of Book II dissects for you a number of ways these defects in your CPU manifest themselves.

So, yes, you're functioning with a dysfunctional model of the world, but unfortunately, the model is necessary for survival. The alternative is paralysis.

Without creating some model of the world, we wouldn't be able to make any decisions, something we're doing every moment of our lives.

Chapter 1: Your Model of the World

Since you started reading this book you made an innumerable number of microdecisions to keep reading this book, and you'll make a great deal more before you finish it and pass this book on to someone else.

Sometimes the decisions we make get us things we want. Sometimes they don't.

Why do we make decisions that are contrary to our wants and desires? Is our model of the world really that defective?

No one knows for sure, but there are many clues. The first is . . .

Belief

Rigid *belief* is a model of the world that creates mental dysfunction.

Because our model of the world will always be incomplete, and therefore fallible, belief in one model or another (without flexibility) can cause us a great deal of pain.

(If you want a great read sometime, *The True Believer* by Eric Hoffer has some insightful ruminations on the mental dysfunction of the believer.)

Is "dysfunction" too strong a word?

Take this incident at Dave's pub.

The bartender at the pub believes this statement: "All Arabs are terrorists."

He's been whipped up into a frenzy by the media and his government's propaganda, and he is now convinced that the crazy Ay-rabs are out to get him.

So, one day a crazy Arab walks into the pub all excited.

> **CRAZY ARAB**
> *(shouts something in Arabic)*

> **BARTENDER**
> What?

> **CRAZY ARAB**
> *(shouts in Arabic even more loudly)*

> **BARTENDER**
> Do any of you guys know what the hell Osama is saying?

> **CRAZY ARAB**
> *(grabs Bartender's shirt and shouts again)*
> *(Bartender reaches down, grabs a baseball bat, and beats Crazy Arab.)*

Was this rational?

Well, if you believe that "all Arabs are terrorists"—why not?

I mean, this guy's an Arab. All Arabs are terrorists. Terrorists kill people. Why else would this guy be shouting?

I wonder what the Arab guy is saying.

In the Bartender's mind, it is probably something like this:

> **CRAZY ARAB**
> Praise be to Allah! You must convert to Islam now, or I will rain a million blows upon you and your family.

> **BARTENDER**
> What?

I mean it! I'm gonna jump across there right now and go 9/11 on yo' ass because you are selling the devil sauce to God's children.

BARTENDER

Do any of you guys know what the hell Osama is saying?

CRAZY ARAB

(grabs the Bartender) Infidel, this is your last chance. I swear to Allah that I'm gonna mess you up—you and all your Yankee imperialist buddies.

(Bartender reaches down, grabs a baseball bat, and beats Crazy Arab.)

Now, if the Bartender doesn't have this belief—or perhaps is more flexible in his beliefs—it's likely he would interpret the events differently.

In this case, Crazy Arab is actually a graphic artist who has just emigrated from Jordan. His wife is outside waiting in the car and going into labor.

The Jordanian can even speak a bit of English, but in the heat of the moment only Arabic comes out.

Really, he is just asking for the nearest hospital or a telephone—whichever is closer.

Depending on your own beliefs, the way you reacted to that last passage will vary as well.

You might think . . .

- If you believe that people who want peace are all hippy freaks:

  "Joyner is a lefty-pinko terrorist apologist. He's one of these guys who tries to see the good in everyone and is just going to get us all in trouble while the enemy walks all over us. This is brainwashing to make us complacent about the growing terrorist threat."

- If you believe that foul language is an offense to God:

  "Joyner has a foul mouth!"

Not only does belief about the world dramatically affect our perception and behavior, our beliefs about ourselves do as well.

For example, you may believe "there is no way I'll ever be rich."

Well, if that's true, then doing things to make yourself rich would just be silly, wouldn't they?

But what if it weren't true? What if there were, in fact, a few relatively foolproof ways to make yourself financially independent?

Holding the belief "I'll never be rich" just closes you off to those possibilities—no matter what the reality is.

It's interesting to note that depending on your belief system, what may appear irrational to some may appear *rational* to you.

Hmmm . . . is what is "rational" dependent upon belief and therefore variable?

Hold that thought for later.

First, let's look at a few of the ways beliefs are formed.

In the case of the Bartender, a number of forces are at play.

When he was young, his daddy always used to say to him, "Son, never trust an Arab. They will burn you every time."

Because of a psychological phenomenon known as "obedience to authority" we tend to believe the words spoken by an authority we respect.

The authority can be anyone really—a parent, a politician, a schoolteacher, a respected friend. But once you put someone in that position of authority, you've also given them a certain amount of control over your mind.

Not only will you tend to believe them, you'll also tend to agree with them and even obey them as well.

How far will people go in obedience?

Well, according to Stanley Milgram, the psychologist who coined the phrase "obedience to authority" with his seminal work of the same title in 1974, pretty damned far.

Milgram once set up an experiment where he "tricked" a number of his test subjects into thinking that they were giving someone a series of electrical shocks of ascending intensity.

When it became clear to the test subjects that the shocks were about to get lethal, the "authority figure" in the experiment assured them that they should proceed with the lethal shocks.

Thirty-seven out of 40 participants gave the lethal shocks.

And this is nothing.

A look at the twentieth century shows how obedience to authority resulted in the largest mass murders in history:

> First Place: Mao Tse-tung
> (50–80 million depending on the source)
>
> First Runner Up: Joseph Stalin
> (22–40 million depending on the source)
>
> *(They didn't kill people themselves. Their obedient followers did the work for them.)*

Did you expect me to say Mao and Stalin?

You were thinking another name, weren't you?

Well, his was actually the third largest mass murder in history, but by far the most "popular." (And asking yourself, Why is that? might be an interesting exercise in belief if you're brave enough to ask.)

Anyway, back to the Bartender.

He is obediently believing what his dad has told him all his childhood and youth, and then in school he learned that the Arabs had actually *invented* numbers and more than a few other useful things.

Chapter 2: Belief

This created a certain amount of . . .

> **Cognitive dissonance** The discomfort felt when two seemingly conflicting ideas are held in the mind.

This phenomenon can propel people forward to the formation of new beliefs, but it can also motivate us to simply make our beliefs even firmer despite evidence to the contrary.

In the Bartender's case it is the latter. He would argue with his professor and constantly look for examples of Arab aggression throughout history to justify his position.

The more he argues, the more he believes.

One of his classmates notices his aggressive hatred of Arabs and invites him to an after-school meeting at his special "club."

The Bartender doesn't have many friends, so he believes this might be a "great opportunity."

The club, it turns out, is a meeting of The Anti-Terrorist Underground. He listens all night to screeds against the Arabs and the seemingly incontrovertible evidence that the Arabs are indeed all planning to convert the planet to Islam. But "the Government" isn't doing enough about it.

"We have to do something about this!"

Every time they angrily spit out the phrase "the Arabs" the Bartender feels warm inside.

The interesting corollary to cognitive dissonance is that when we learn things that are in support of our beliefs, they make us feel good.

After all—the opposite of dissonance is *harmony*.

After the meetings, many of the members go out for drinks together and share additional stories.

There is hardly any disagreement in the conversations that take place thereafter.

They start to show signs of:

> **Groupthink** The phenomenon whereby the belief of an individual will conform to the perceived beliefs of a group—even if otherwise irrational, unhealthy, or dangerous.

The phenomenon is also described as the psychological phenomenon of "conformity to group norms."

By the end of his days at the university, the Bartender is a "true believer."

Now, the preceding story, while fantasy, isn't too far removed from the kind of thing that happens every day around the world.

The names, the beliefs, and the groups are all interchangeable.

While this example is extreme, the same dynamics are at play to greater or lesser degrees in *all* of us.

Dare you examine your own beliefs and the way they are formed?

That notion probably makes you at least mildly uncomfortable.

Why is that?

Do our beliefs serve us in some way?

Well, sometimes they do, and sometimes they don't.

Either way, understanding them gives us *flexibility* and therefore more control over our lives. And conscious awareness of these various forces tends to lessen their effects.

Now, this chapter is certainly by no means an exhaustive look at the mechanism of belief formation, but it's a start.

More insights might be formed with a study of . . .

Influence

Is it possible to control the behavior of others?

What would you do if you had that power? And what if that power were in the hands of your country?

The search for perfect mind control has seduced many over the years and has been the justification for some rather sadistic crimes.

The CIA's MK Ultra mind control experiments are a dandy example.

Yes, in the 1950s the CIA did in fact experiment with drugs, electronic signals, and various other cool gadgets for use in the manipulation of human behavior.

Apparently we feared the "the enemy" (then the Soviet Union and China) was doing the same thing.

Hey, if they're doin' it, we better do it, too.

Right?

Dr. Sidney Gottlieb, the director of the program, was known to have drugged many MK Ultra test subjects with LSD, locked them into isolation chambers, and played back recordings of them saying their most self-degrading statements over and over again.

It might sound like a lot of conspiracy theory craziness, but the Freedom of Information Act has made it quite clear that these experiments were in fact "real."

**Anti-American Wacko or
Pro-America Patriot?**

The belief systems of some of the people reading this might make them think that my mention of MK Ultra makes me an anti-American wacko.

"A true patriot would not remind the world of America's failings," they might say.

They might also want to take into consideration that I served in the U.S. Army for almost a decade and that I actually *believe* in the value of the American message "liberty and justice for all."

Talking about this actually doesn't make me unpatriotic even if today's political climate might paint me as such. (Don't criticize. We're at war, I tell you!) And it also doesn't put me on one side, either.

I imagine that various people reading this book so far have me pegged as any number of colors across the political spectrum. Which of them is right? You'll know by the time you read the rest of this book.

58

Book II: The Invisible Walls

While all of this may sound rather spooky, there are more mundane forms of mind control being practiced every day.

In fact, it's happening *to* you and *by* you on a regular basis.

But we don't call it "mind control." We give it different names:

> When it's used by companies to influence you to purchase a product, it's called "marketing."
>
> When it's used by a politician of your own country, it might be called a "speech."
>
> If the same speech is given by "the enemy," it might then be called "propaganda."
>
> If it's used by a father on his children it might be called "gentle persuasion."
>
> If it's the spirited words of a coach before the big game it might be called a "pep talk."

And before you point fingers and play the victim, remember that you're actively engaged in this process as well. Have you ever tried to convince a group of people to see a particular film or eat at a particular restaurant?

That's influence.

On any given day your mind is bombarded with hundreds of forms of influence.

> Some of it you're conscious of; some of it you're not.
>
> Without seeing it, it passes into your mind and has an effect.
>
> Even if you see it, if you don't know how to properly evaluate it, it will have an effect.

What's an"effect?" Well, if your aim is to get from point A to point B, and a form of influence persuades you to get to Point Z, this takes you further away from what you want.

The Invisible Walls get clearer. . . .

What exactly *is* influence, then?

Have we actually "cracked the code" of persuasion?

Through all of this experimentation have we discovered a way to control human behavior without locking subjects into isolation chambers and humiliating them on acid?

A great many people have attempted to answer this question and virtually none of them agree, despite some striking similarities.

However, there are some extremely useful "models of persuasion" that are stunningly effective if understood.

Before you dismiss any of this, you should probably be aware that there are a great many people out there making a deliberate study of these ideas.

Why? Because they want an *edge* in their attempts to control you.

Anyone who has worked in a marketing department or on a political campaign knows that this isn't just paranoid rambling.

There are two general approaches to persuasion study that seem to be common.

Conceptual Models

These models attempt to break persuasion down into a number of rules or laws.

The best of these might be that of Robert Cialdini. His essential book *Influence* is an exhaustive study of the mechanisms of influence in a very scientific and, well, persuasive way.

Among the serious academic attempts to understand persuasion and influence Cialdini's is perhaps the best known.

Drawing on the work of many of the psychologists mentioned throughout this book and many others, he studied the practitioners of influence in great detail—from the salesperson trying to sell you a car to the Hare Krishna in the airport tricking you into buying his book.

Cialdini describes for us six distinct "weapons" of influence:

1. *Reciprocation*   If someone feels that someone has given them something, they are at times compelled to give in return.

2. *Commitment and Consistency*   If people make commitments either verbal or perceived, they tend to feel compelled to keep them. Further, people tend to feel compelled to remain consistent with their past behaviors.

3. *Social Proof*   Remember "groupthink" and "conformity to group norms?" Same stuff here—except now we're talking about the deliberate use of this

phenomenon to purposely change behavior. (Interesting how the same dynamics apply, isn't it?)

4. *Liking* It is easier for people we like to influence our behavior.

5. *Authority* Remember "obedience to authority?"

6. *Scarcity* If we feel that our chance to do something will not exist in the future, we're more likely to do it in the now.

Formulaic Models

Formulaic models tend to break persuasion down into step-by-step or mathematical formulas, rather than concepts.

Among my friends are some of the most dangerous teachers of influence in the world. Most of them are armed with years of study and practical application of the various weapons of influence (in addition to the more academic approaches, most have also mastered the more esoteric forms of persuasion like Neurolinguistic Programming and hypnosis).

I'm loath to even mention these guys in the same breath as MK Ultra because while they are persuasion masters, most of them are also what I'd categorize as "good people." They teach persuasion mainly to businesses in order to help them improve sales.

Like anything else, these concepts can be used for good or evil.

Not every persuader has your best interests in mind.

At the same time, not everyone wielding influence is out to get you.

Either way, learning from teachers of influence and marketers will free your mind and alert you to when these tactics are being used against you. This gives you options.

Among these friends is Dr. Kevin Hogan. He's a genius at what he does.

I asked Dr. Hogan, "What is your ultimate persuasion formula?" His excellent reply is presented below.

10 Simple Steps I Use to Persuade Anyone

Dr. Kevin Hogan

1. Determine and control the context. People respond and react (unconsciously) very differently in different settings. (Think of your behavior in a library, hospital waiting room, sports stadium, McDonald's, elegant restaurant.)

   Places: We also react differently around different people, morphing some of their personality into ours and vice versa. So, when you communicate with someone, who else is around who is going to influence your client's decision, other than you?

   (Continued)

Things: If I have a copy of *Maxim* or *FHM* on my coffee table, you will respond differently from if I have *Time, Newsweek,* and *BusinessWeek.* All of the things in the environment including the clothes on you persuade.

2. *Determine my outcome.* My desired outcome must be mutually beneficial with my client's. What specifically do I want to happen? What is my target?

3. *Empathize.* You can't influence if you don't have empathy. In most cases, the people I persuade become my friends. I want to find out and feel out who my client is . . . what their desires, drives, wants, and motivators are.

4. *Defuse resistance.* Reaction and resistance is normal to each persuasion attempt. Expect it. Defuse major resistance by pointing out a flaw in yourself. I make fun of myself, I show imperfections in products. People don't go searching for what you have already shown them.

5. *Defuse feelings of anticipated regret.* "If I buy this I'm going to regret it. . . ."

    You need to take people on a time travel to the future and show how it *is* possible they could regret it, but then paint the more likely scenario that your product/service will give them what they want.

6. *Frame proposal.* The mortality rate of surgery A is 20 percent. The chances of living through surgery B are 80 percent. Which surgery do you want to have? Of course B—except they are the same—yet the frame of one sentence costs people their lives every day. Think carefully of how you want to frame your proposal.

7. *Propose.* Propose a solution that might be the desired outcome. But first offer an alternative choice that is inferior for some almost obvious reason. *Then* offer your option and move forward with certainty that the person has accepted it.

8. *Solve obstacles that exist.* In advance. Most persuaders try to think of comebacks. That's wild. You should have long ago thought about every possible path the communication could have taken. Presolve all possible obstacles. Then, *do not* solve them too quickly, or you make the client look foolish or stupid.

9. *Ask until they say yes.*

10. *Validate later.* Know that after they have said yes, they will experience near instant regret for a few days. This is true whether the woman is picking one man over another or choosing one car over another. You must validate the person's decision. Not immediately after the consummation of the deal but a day later.

From Dr. Kevin Hogan, http://www.kevinhogan.com

What you've just read is only a small sampling of the information that has been amassed for the purpose of manipulating and controlling you.

More about Frames

Dr. Hogan touched on them briefly in his formula. In fact, I tend to believe that "the frame" is the most powerful persuasion concept in existence.

It may even serve as a valid "uber principle" under which all other persuasion principles can be organized. That is, it's possible to look at virtually all persuasion principles as one form of "frame manipulation" or another.

What is frame manipulation?

First, you must know that the frame is "the information around the information." It can be anything.

In the same way the frame around a painting affects the way it appears, the frame around information largely determines how you see and interpret that information.

For example, you'd be more likely to think a painting is a work of fine art if you saw it hanging in the Louvre.

If you saw the same painting on the street sold by a shabby looking vagrant, you'd be likely to dismiss it.

Another frame around that same piece of art could be the opinion of an expert you hear uttered before, after, or while you are viewing it.

Another frame might be the opinions uttered by a group about the painting and any perceived consensus of the group opinion.

Wait, didn't we talk about this before?

We sure did. Again, it's interesting to point out that in one sense, all forms of influence can be explained as various manipulations of someone's frame.

While some shun the study of persuasion ("I don't want to learn how to manipulate people!"), they are only leaving themselves vulnerable to those who do.

Here's a crash course in making yourself invulnerable: The ultimate way to protect yourself from influence is through skepticism and not allowing rapport to affect your thinking.

Easier said than done! Especially when you don't have an understanding of the Invisible Walls formed by . . .

68

Book II: The Invisible Walls

Language

As we learned earlier, language has a subtle, and sometimes mysterious, way of shaping our model of the world.

Dave, for example, is a member of The Giveusyourmoney Party (the G Party) in the United States.

As a dedicated card-carrying member of The Party, he has an instant dislike for anyone who is a member of the other major party: The Pleasegiveusyourmoney Party.

Now, at the local pub . . .

BAR RAT #1

You can't tell me that The G Party is right in supporting the evil occupations of Wewantyourlandia.

DAVE

Of course I do. Wewantyourlandia is our ally and the G Party always supports its allies.

Now, Dave has never had that notion before. He just made that up on the spot for the sake of the argument. (Come on, you know you've done it.)

Over time Dave begins using that phrase more and more in his speech and before he knows it, he *believes* it. (Repetition is a great belief builder. Especially if the repetition is voluntary.)

Now, later on Dave discovers that Wewantyourlandia is not just involved in the illegal occupation of foreign territory, but that it is harassing the residents of the occupied land in unforgivable ways. "Oppression" isn't too harsh a word to describe what they are doing.

When the topic of the United States giving military aid to Wewantyourlandia comes up again, Dave is bound by this language he has cooked up:

"The G Party always supports its allies."

Part of him is very uncomfortable (remember cognitive dissonance), but he has to stick to his guns (remember commitment and consistency).

Not only does this make him feel uncomfortable every time he has to defend his position, it gets in the way of many of his relationships.

Many of his friends who are quite aware of Wewantyourlandia's shenanigans just can't understand his irrational defense of Wewantyourlandia, and it makes his friends lose respect for Dave.

If only Dave understood how he has trapped himself.

Most of us have no knowledge of the way in which language does this, so we have no way of controlling the effects.

Sometimes we can find ourselves in linguistic traps and end up fighting battles that we don't really believe in.

Invisible Walls, indeed.

Not only does this give us less control over ourselves, but it can transfer that control to others. Failing to understand the mechanisms of language makes us ripe for influence.

That same phrase concocted by Dave, if uttered by a politician and accepted by Dave *as is*, would have a similar effect.

And the effects on Dave, whether initiated by him or by someone else, could be even more far-reaching.

As Dave gets deeper into these arguments he begins to use angry language about the opposing party.

Not such a big deal?

Hey, they're only words, right?

Maybe not.

As you will observe for yourself in a moment, the language you use can have an actual physiological impact on your body.

Try this:

> Pick an object on the floor (or ground, wherever you are) and stare at it. *Think* this silently over and over at the object 20 times:
>
> *I hate you*.
>
> Go ahead and try it.

After 20 rounds, how did you feel?

> Now try it again, this time with a great big smile on your face.
>
> Take a second now to do this and come back.

So, what did you notice?

You probably found that the simple act of thinking *I hate you* over and over again didn't make you feel very good. This could have manifested itself in many different ways.

You probably also found that it was uncomfortable/strange to do this with a big smile on your face. (Unless of course you're a bit crazy.)

As you can see, the mere thought of these words doesn't feel so good. The effect of uttering them out loud with conviction would be even more intense.

> Now, to counteract what you just did, please redo both steps of this little experiment and this time say
>
> *I love you*.
>
> Please come back when you've finished.

Now, you'll probably notice that you feel a lot better.

You'll also notice I ended this experiment on that note because I want you to feel good as you read the rest of this book.

Now, no one can say for sure why language has this effect on us. It could be the way these words are networked-up in your brain with certain thoughts and feelings (see the Chapter 12 on Neural Networking). It could be something else.

Many popular new age gurus even say that the words themselves have a physical effect on you and that "quantum physics proves it." (There are more than a few quantum physicists out there who may not agree with that.)

No one knows this for sure (I'll show you how to spot the difference between a crackpot and a real scientist shortly; you are likely to be surprised by what you find).

Either way, you can observe the effect for yourself.

What you may not have observed in the preceding experiment was a sneaky bit of manipulative language I used on you.

Do you remember reading this?

> *You probably also found that it was uncomfortable/ strange to do this with a big smile on your face. (Unless of course you're a bit crazy.)*

Did you catch it?

Probably not. In fact, most of the seasoned persuaders and influencers I know don't have a full grasp of the concept I'm about to teach you.

Now, no matter how you found trying to smile while saying "I hate you" (it is quite likely that it was in fact awkward), your perception and belief that it was awkward was greatly enhanced by the parenthetical sentence that followed it:

(Unless of course you're a bit crazy.)

See, after reading that statement, most people would find it quite hard to disagree with what was said before it.

I mean *you're* not crazy, right?

Hey, what just happened there?

It's imperceptible to the untrained eye. It might be a bit subtle even to the initiated.

What's special and tricky about that statement is that it *presupposes* something else.

Presuppositions (along with double binds and other linguistic tricks) are used by cunning influencers all the time. (Thanks to Kenrick Cleveland for first teaching me this years ago.)

> **Presupposition** The *implicit* assumption behind any explicit statement.

What does that mean?

Well, the statement "unless of course you're a bit crazy" *presupposes* that the following statement is also true:

"Anyone who doesn't feel uncomfortable while simultaneously smiling and saying, 'I hate you' is crazy."

My use of "of course" also reinforced this.

I mean, you're not *stupid*, are you? Of course you want to agree with me.

See there—I did it again. I presupposed that you'd be stupid to disagree with me. Using "of course" the way I did had the same presupposition but was far subtler—*and therefore more effective!*

You may or may not grasp how powerful this concept is yet.

(By the way, for fun, see if you can pick out the presuppositions in the preceding sentence.)

Here is another example that might make this clearer.

Flip ahead to the cartoon on page 127, that includes the phrase "we must deter them from future violence."

What a subtle and powerful communication! (And one often used to justify all manner of aggressive horror.)

When used to justify the attack of another country, it presupposes:

- That our attacks our justified.
- That an attack can serve as a valid way of deterring future violence.
- That our attacks specifically will have this effect.

And most listeners will instantly accept all three of these presupposed statements without thinking.

Whether the statements are true is not what's on your mind.

See, in order to understand the surface meaning of a statement, we must presuppose unconsciously that any implied statements in the language are true.

Now, in an earlier chapter I talked about my walk to work every morning in Auckland, New Zealand.

While reading it, you may have painted a picture in your mind that presupposed many things:

- There is an office building in New Zealand where I work.
- I can walk.
- There is a place called Auckland in New Zealand.

It's a statistical probability that you have never actually been there (knowing what I know about my likely readers, the population of the world, and the frequency of New Zealand as a tourist destination). So, how do you actually *know* it exists?

You didn't question a single one of those things, did you?

They all happen to be true, but I could have easily placed some egregiously untrue statements in that list and you would not have batted an eye.

The beauty (and danger) of the presupposition as a persuasive tool is that it bypasses your judgment. Even if you have

Chapter 4: Language

hardened yourself with skepticism and are selective about rapport, such statements fly right past your radar and right into your brain.

These Invisible Walls may be appearing more real now.

Let's dig even deeper.

In the case of the "deterrence" cartoon on page 127, some readers may have a rather strong opinion to the contrary about the underlying presuppositions therein. Depending on their sensitivity to language, this preformed opinion can have many effects.

An extremely deft and experienced communicator might say:

> "Your statement is based on an underlying presupposition that I believe to be false. Namely *(fill in the presupposition here)*."
>
> (It might serve you well to memorize this phrase.)

But even a well-educated and otherwise extremely intelligent person is unlikely to have this level of linguistic mastery.

An educated person with an opinion to the contrary is likely to simply feel an amount of extreme discomfort while reading those words. They'll feel that "something is wrong" with what was just said, but in the heat of the moment (watching a speech, arguing politics), they're extremely unlikely to unravel it.

It's too much for the brain to handle.

The effect of this is so strong that it's even possible to change someone's opinion on the fly. The person with the changed opinion would probably feel tremendously uncomfortable at first, but they might feel compelled to express a minor agreement.

"Yes, that may be true, but . . ."

Well, now they've said it once and "commitment and consistency" is likely to kick in from there.

And then another phenomenon, perhaps best summed up by an old marketing truism comes into play:

"We base our decisions on emotion and justify them with logic."

Well, as you've just learned, emotion is but one of many of the unconscious factors in forming beliefs and making decisions, but you get the idea.

The human brain is expert at coming up with logical justifications for past actions and existing opinions—even if they were formed unconsciously.

So, how do we take back command of our language?

It starts with the awareness that:

> *"The map is not the territory."*
> —Alfred Korzybski

Remember that the words we use to communicate are separate from the things/concepts we are using those words to describe.

Not only are they separate, but like our mental model of the world they are also by definition:

- Incomplete
- Imprecise
- Distorted

The improbability of effective communication is underscored thus:

Imagine a near-blind man trying to describe what he sees to an English speaker in Swahili.

To a lesser degree (and some may argue only slightly lesser) that is an apt description of our everyday communication.

How is that so? Three ways:

1. What we're seeing is an incomplete and distorted picture.
2. The words we use to describe what we see are imprecise.
3. The interpretation of those words by the listener will always be at least slightly different from the intended meaning. (Words mean different things to different people based on their mental model.)

The day they decided that Sneetches are Sneetches.
And no kind of Sneetch is the best on the beaches.
That day, all the Sneetches forgot about stars and whether
They had one, or not, upon thars.

And still we can hear someone say, "Oh, you're a member of the Democratic Party, too?" and feel a deep connection with them.

Now, many people after first learning these concepts feel a certain amount of helplessness. Don't. I'm about to throw you a lifeline, but that feeling will get worse before it gets better.

Name-Calling

This is a special subset of language that really deserves its own book, or perhaps even a university degree, but we'll just have to settle for this short chapter.

Here's another conversation Dave had at the pub while in his "card-carrying-member-of-the-G-Party" phase.

PUB RAT #9
Man, I'm not so sure about what our government is doing right now.

DAVE
Oh, jeez. Here we go again. What's your gripe this time?

PUB RAT #9
Well, I don't understand why we're about to go to war with Wegotlotsaoilya. What did they do to us?

DAVE
Are you crazy!? Their leader is a maniac and has sworn to destroy us.

PUB RAT #9

Actually he hasn't ever said that. It's a common mis-translation.

DAVE

Whatever. Pill O'Crazy said it best: We absolutely *must* attack them for our security!

PUB RAT #9

But isn't it a fact that their president who's in power is there because we put in a brutal dictator before him? I mean, that's why they had a revolution, right? They actually had a democratically elected leader before, but we used the CIA to stage a coup in order to prevent them from nationalizing their oil.

DAVE

Dude, what's wrong with you?! Aren't you a patriot? I can't believe you're defending those guys! How can you possibly side with the enemy?

What Pub Rat #9 actually said is true, but he doesn't know how to respond to Dave. He is frozen.

Dave doesn't hear a word Pub Rat says, though. If he listened to #9, he might learn something, but with some judicious name-calling he shuts down any possibility of intelligent discussion.

What happened?

Here are the two most important names hurled:

"Patriot"
"The Enemy"

We might be able to write a whole Ph.D. dissertation on the power of these words, but here's a start.

First, they are both emotionally charged. Close your eyes and think about each word individually. How do they make you feel?

"Patriot" might makes you feel warm and fuzzy inside. You might see your country's flag and chiseled sculptures of war heroes of yore.

"The Enemy" might conjure up images of war propaganda or even nefarious alien invaders.

When we are emotionally roused, it's difficult for us to think or behave rationally. Emotion-laden language in general can have this effect on us, but there's more to name-calling.

In this case, the names are combined with the power of pre-suppositions for devastating effect.

That is, Dave's diatribe presupposes many things. Here are two important ones:

1. Wegotlotsaoilya is our "enemy."
2. If you bring any evidence forward that might reflect favorably on "the enemy" you are not a Patriot.

But the real insidious thing here is that it creates a very subtle double bind, that is:

You are either going to agree with me, or you're not a Patriot.

And another:

> You are going to agree with me or side with The Enemy.

Since #9 doesn't have the linguistic tools available to dissect this (*you* will by the end of Book III), he has no choice but to stop arguing.

However, he isn't happy about it.

Why? Because of consistency: He doesn't want to say that he is wrong, but he also doesn't want to not be a Patriot.

This kind of mental collapse can cause fistfights or worse.

Yet another way name-calling works with consistency to warp our minds comes from the names we call ourselves.

Look at this statement:

> "I'm a Christian Scientist."

Whatever definition you have for Christian Scientist in your mind would probably include a number of various traits.

These traits may not be traits you yourself possess, but once you give yourself that label, it is very likely you'd start to adopt them.

Not only does it change your behavior when you label yourself, but it changes the way you perceive others when you label *them*.

Why?

Labels are, by definition, inherently wrong.

If you grasp the full implications of that sentence, you may wonder, "Is that really true?"

In a few chapters it will be made quite clear that it is.

Meanwhile, here is yet another Invisible Wall that is particularly hard to overcome because it is rooted in your inherently and chronically. . . .

Chapter 5: Name-Calling

Faulty Thinking

Even if we have mastered language and are sensitive to influence, we can still draw invalid conclusions from what we observe and hear.

Let's revisit Dave in the pub.

He is arguing with Bar Rat #1 about the existence of God.

Dave, among other things, is an atheist.

Bar Rat #1 believes in the Christian God.

> **BAR RAT #1**
> How can you not believe in God, man? I mean, what do you think happens when you die? Do you think you just cease to exist?
>
> **DAVE**
> Yes. Yes, I do. It's a sad, unfortunate existential state of affairs, but that's the reality.

BAR RAT #1

That's pretty sad, man.

DAVE

It's sad, but the fact is, you're basing your belief on a book you read. You don't actually *know* God exists.

BAR RAT #1

Okay, well answer me a question.

DAVE

Shoot.

BAR RAT #1

Do you believe that George Washington was the first president?

DAVE

Of course.

BAR RAT #1

Uh huh, and how do you know this?

DAVE

It's in every book I've read!

BAR RAT #1

In books, huh?

DAVE

But that's not the same!

BAR RAT #1

Uh huh, whatever. Thank you for proving my point.

Well, he is right. Dave did form his beliefs on "just a book" as well, but he feels something is wrong in that comparison but can't put his finger on it.

The Fool comes in the next day and Dave asks him for advice.

THE FOOL

Good lord, man, hasn't anyone taught you about logical fallacies?

DAVE

What's that?

THE FOOL

That explains a lot.

DAVE

Well, enlighten me then!

THE FOOL

Okay, think about it. Does the conclusion Bar Rat made logically follow?

DAVE

What do you mean?

THE FOOL

Break it down. His argument is something to the effect that

- The bible says God exists.
- The bible is a book.
- You based your belief on a book.
- Therefore, you have to believe in God—the conclusion of *my* book.

DAVE

What's wrong with that?

THE FOOL

Well, let's see if we can fill in the blanks with something to make it untrue. For example, would you agree with this statement?

- The book *Star Wars* says that Darth Vader is Luke Skywalker's father.
- The *Star Wars* book is a book.

91

Chapter 6: Faulty Thinking

- You based your belief on a book.
- Therefore, you have to believe that Darth Vader truly is Luke Skywalker's father.

DAVE

Ah, I think I'm getting it.

The Fool goes on to explain that the study of logical fallacies identifies a number of common, incorrect thought patterns.

Bar Rat #1 is guilty of an "invalid syllogism." (Remember this, it will come in handy in Book III. . . .)

At other times in other arguments, Bar Rat #1 is guilty of:

Appeal to ignorance A logical fallacy in which *lack* of proof to the contrary is put forth as proof to the affirmative. "Absence of evidence is not evidence of absence."

Bar Rat would say:

"You have no evidence that God doesn't exist. Therefore, God exists."

But, by using the same faulty logic, one could argue:

"Life on other planets does not exist. Never, through thousands of years of research and study by the revered scientists, have we been able to produce a single shred of evidence to suggest that life exists outside of Earth. Not NASA. Not Einstein. No one."

It sounds pretty persuasive.

It's also unadulterated horse crap.

Not only is the statement using appeal to ignorance, it is also using another common logical fallacy called

> **Appeal to authority**   A logical fallacy in which the support of a position by a particular authority figure is proof of its validity.

Of course, authorities are humans with faulty models just like you and therefore fallible.

Therefore, basing an argument on an appeal to authority is *fallacious*.

DAVE

This is great!

THE FOOL

Yeah, it's powerful stuff.

(They tap beer bottles.)

DAVE

You know, man, it's good to have someone on my side who is also an atheist. It's so hard to explain this stuff to these morons.

THE FOOL

Actually man, I'm a Christian.

Another all too common fallacy is:

> **Post hoc ergo propter hoc**   (*Latin: After this therefore because of this*.) A logical fallacy in which it is assumed that because one event occurs after another, the precedent event is the cause.

93

Chapter 6: Faulty Thinking

Well, what's wrong with that? If something happens after something else, isn't it safe to assume you know the *cause?*

Let's imagine that you drank some milk. An hour later you have a stomach ache.

Bad milk?

Many would jump to this conclusion, but of course it's not necessarily a valid one. Any number of things could have caused the stomach upset (something else you ate, something you inhaled, and so on).

Most of us can see this example quite clearly and think, "Well, I'm not likely to make *that* mistake."

Don't be so sure.

A common argument you hear on television "news" programs (I put "news" in quotes because much of what is passed off as objective news today is arguably bona fide propaganda) is as follows:

> Ever since President Promiseyoutheworld took office the economy has been a shambles! How can you possibly say he is a good president? Don't you have any concern for the future of our children?! How can you urge people to vote for this man in good conscience?!

Of course, we don't know that the "bad economy" was in fact *caused* by this president; it could have been caused by a lot of things.

There are other problems with the statement as well. Do you sense what they are?

A good linguist or logistician would have a field day picking it apart.

The exercise would be extremely useful but might take us off target. For now, here's just one more clue:

> **Appeal to emotion**   An argument that uses emotion, rather than logic, to persuade the listener.

Just because someone feels strongly about something doesn't make it so.

But this kind of emotional browbeating is quite common.

It's amazing how frequently it is used on news programs that are supposed to be sober and fair.

It's interesting to note that these fallacies are yet another form of influence. The persuader will rely on your ignorance of logic and use that to trick you.

Next time you watch a political speech or a news commentator, see if you can pick up on the fallacies used.

Most people aren't thinking like this. They are watching it happen, but they are unconsciously affected without an understanding of the mechanisms at play.

These are but a few of the many different fallacies that have been identified over the years.

There are many others and you'd do well to master them.

Fallacies

The best resource I've ever found on this topic (and I'd make this a regular visit if I were you) is the following web site:

http://www.fallacyfiles.org

Not only does the site give the most exhaustive list of fallacies I've ever seen, it has categorized them into a unique hierarchical taxonomy of fallacies.

You won't master them in a sitting, so occasionally dipping into that web site will give you greater and greater mastery of the world around you.

Pseudoscience

What do you get when you mix influence with faulty thinking?

> **Pseudoscience** A body of knowledge that has the outward appearance of science, but does not genuinely rely on the scientific method—instead, often relying on faith.

What Does Pseudoscience Look Like?

Back in the Wild West days con artists would sell bottles of snake oil to "cure all that ails ya" from the back of roving wagons.

The wagons moved from town to town so that the public wouldn't be able to ask for their money back once they realized they had been duped.

Doctors with dubious credentials, scientific studies that never actually existed . . . These are some of the various trappings of science used to dupe people into thinking that the products were valid.

The snake oil peddlers of today are far more sophisticated.

Fake science is still their primary weapon, but they wrap it with a few other devious tools of persuasion to enhance the effect.

For example, instead of presenting a doctor as the figure of authority, they may present an "all-knowing spirit," channeled by the huckster.

The power of such a tactic is sinister.

The wisdom of mere mortals may be up for debate, but the wisdom of a super spirit? Who dares question!

Once you accept that the super spirit is telling the truth . . .

. . . *a not-so-difficult feat after they have uttered a few warm platitudes to get you nodding your head in agreement* . . .

. . . you will then tend to accept everything they say as true. Once you've done that, you've basically given up all decision making and authority you once possessed to the huckster claiming to channel the great spirit.

Of course you'll buy their tape sets and their magic beans.

Another earmark of today's pseudoscience is a reliance on belief.

That is, much of the pseudo-scientific claptrap of today comes with the claim that "you must believe" (or have faith) in order for it to work.

Hmm, is there anything wrong with that?

Let's find out. . . .

How Pseudoscience Rapes Your Mind

One day, Dave took a jaunt to a local new age store:

DAVE

(Picks up shiny object) Hey, what's this?

HIS HOLINESS

That's a Dual Universal Harmonizing Protector Chip, or DUHP (pronounced *dupe*) Chip for short. It is known to cure every illness known to man. It'll also improve your tennis game!

DAVE

Sounds pretty high-tech.

HH

It is. It's based on quantum physics!

DAVE

Wow, so it's pretty scientific?

HH

It sure is. It's based on our newer understanding of "the laws of the universe."

DAVE

Wow, I didn't know there were laws of the universe! Maybe that's what I've been missing. So do you have some scientific studies that show it works?

HH

Ha! You understand very little of the laws of the universe. Why do you need a scientific study for everything? Did your mother beat you when you were a child?

DAVE

I thought you said it was scientific.

HH

It doesn't work like that. You have much to learn. This chip was created based on the theories of Dr. Iwantyourmoolah in the mountains of Pakistan—the most revered quantum physicist in the world! Paris Hilton has one, and another for her dog.

DAVE

Okay, I guess I'll try one.

So Dave took his DUHP Chip home and tried it out. As instructed, he wore it strapped to his head (enduring the laughter of his pubmates) and seemed to feel "a little better."

The DUHP Chip must work!

A few weeks later, he caught a cold.

So, he strapped on his trusty DUHP Chip, sure that it would "cure" him.

A few days passed and he was still sick.

So, he went back into the new age store:

DAVE

I think my DUHP Chip is broken. I have been sick for three days and it doesn't seem to be helping.

HH

(*Examines it*) There's nothing wrong with the DUHP Chip—the problem must be the way you are using it.

DAVE

But, I followed the instructions.

HH

Well, did you have any negative thoughts?

DAVE

Hmm. Yeah, I guess so.

HH

You fool! The DUHP Chip is a magnifier of your thoughts on the *quantum* level! If you wear the DUHP Chip when you have negative thoughts, it could *kill* you for real!

DAVE

Oh no, what have I done!

101

Chapter 7: Pseudoscience

I have another product that will help you banish your negative thoughts.

DAVE

Oh, thank you. Thank you.

So, Dave tried his new positive thinking product and sure enough a few days later his cold was gone. (Of course, the cold just ran its course, but Dave thought it was because of his trusty DUHP Chip and his positive thinking.)

A year later Dave was diagnosed with cancer.

He went back to the store and asked for help.

DAVE

I swear my thinking has been positive!

HH

Well, perhaps you think it is, but it's not. I've seen it happen many times.

DAVE

I swear I've been thinking positively. I swear. Are you sure your laws of the universe are right?

HH

What! How dare you question the laws of the universe? They are inflexible. They have existed since time immemorial. Every scientist alive agrees with them. It is not the laws that are wrong, it is your *thinking* that is wrong. I think you need to attend our positive thinking boot camp.

Now, you might read this and say, "What's wrong with positive thinking! It couldn't hurt!"

Well, that may be true. In fact, there is some interesting evidence out there that suggests that our thoughts may in fact have an impact on our health.

So, what's the problem?

Well, first of all, we don't know to what extent this is true.

That is, it may be that our thoughts have an even larger impact on the outside world and on our health than we have even imagined.

Or . . .

It may be that they affect our health in minor ways, but the mechanisms are not yet understood.

Or . . .

It may be none of these things at all. We just don't know.

Despite that we don't know, many of the people teaching "positive thinking," "law of attraction," and the like do so in an inflexible and dogmatic way.

There's nothing wrong with positive thinking per se, but there is a problem with an inflexible dogmatic model of the world—especially when that model itself is likely to result in some truly harmful decisions (like putting your trust in a dodgy new age gadget when your health is on the line).

And again, many of these devices and products require you to have faith or to use "the power of your mind" to have any effect.

So, *is* that so bad? What's wrong with faith?

Two things:

First, you could say "it's faith" about anything. I could go find wood chips in my yard and sell them as Quantum Naturizers and then explain that they work only if you believe they will.

That's not science—it's faith.

It's also outright fraud if you know that your product itself doesn't have any effect and you claim that it does.

Second, if it *is* faith, people just need to *say* that it's faith. What they're selling is religion, but they are calling it science.

Why not just be honest?

It's a good question. The purveyors of these products put so much time into weaving their deceptive looms—they obviously have not yet figured out that they could put the same time and energy into developing a product that actually works and make a lot more money in the long run.

Maybe that's not the whole picture, though. Some of these guys may actually believe their crackpot science.

I wonder if these guys do. . . .

Case Study: What the Baloney—a Tour de Force of Pseudoscience

An even subtler form of pseudoscience is the deliberate distortion, or misinterpretation, of otherwise good science.

David Albert, Ph.D. (professor of Philosophy and director of the M.A. program in "The Philosophical Foundations of

Physics" at Columbia University), accuses the cult film *What the Bleep Do We Know!?* of doing this.

What's most shocking about this is that Dr. Albert is actually featured in the film and his comments (edited to his disliking) are included in the film to support the view proposed by *What the Bleep!?*

But, of course, those who watch the film walk away thinking that they have a deep understanding of quantum physics that is widely agreed upon by scientific authorities throughout the globe.

If you peer deeper you find that much of the "science" presented as "fact" in the film is what many consider to be junk science without double-blind studies or peer review.

Dig even deeper and you'll find that one of the oh-so-authoritative figures is a woman named J.Z. Knight.

Oh, wait—I mean Ramtha.

See, it's not Knight who is the authority, but the age-old superbeing Knight claims to channel: Ramtha, of whom the creators of the film are devotees.

According to Ramtha, the "old way" of seeing the world is wrong and this "new way" is right, and by golly we've got a parade of experts echoing this belief to prove it.

Now, surely many fans of this film will be annoyed with me poking fun. Am I being unfair?

Let's see. . . .

One seemingly implied idea of the film—that you can cure yourself of illness by writing positive words on your body— might even be irresponsibly dangerous.

Note: In the lawsuit *Knight* vs. *Knight*, her ex-husband (J.Z.'s, not Ramtha's; I better be careful here lest I get sued myself) claimed that he put off years of traditional AIDS treatment because he believed the ancient healing methods of J.Z. (oops, I mean Ramtha) would cure him. We'll never know because he's dead now (of, you guessed it, AIDS complications). "He must have stopped having faith too soon. Perhaps if he had just believed a little bit more. . . ." (I can hear the Ramtha followers say.)

Hey, I'd love for *that* to work!

I'd be one writing-on-your-body fool if it did, but does it?

If you are among those who think it does, let's test your faith.

If you come down with a life-threatening illness, will you attempt to cure yourself in this way before seeking other treatment? (Not that the medical community doesn't have its share of colossal mistakes—especially when it relies on drugs to cure rather than good habits to prevent—but if you need a triple bypass are you gonna call up Ramtha? Or a heart surgeon who has performed the procedure successfully 1,000 times?)

Let's just be blunt: Some of the conclusions that are "proven by science" in *What the Bleep!?* are pure faith masquerading as science.

Two examples:

First, let's take the conclusion that your brain manufactures reality out of nothing.

The film presents some of the genuinely bizarre and interesting conundrums of quantum physics and then makes some rather ambitious leaps of faith.

For example, the famous "dual-slit experiment" and others indicate that an *observer* may in fact have an effect on what is being observed. (Stuff for you to Google at your leisure: Copenhagen interpretation, dual-slit experiment, Schrodinger's Cat).

What the Bleep!? presents these experiments as "proof" that we create our own reality.

The mysteries of the universe solved!

The reality is that these experiments present more questions than answers.

There are many divergent interpretations of the dual-slit experiment, and some suspect it is simply an artifact or limitation of the currently available methods of measurement and observation.

Hey, maybe we *do* create our own reality, but let's not fool ourselves that scientists around the world believe this is so. (And let's similarly stand up to the demagogues who try to browbeat us with pseudoscience into believing it.)

The real problem with this notion is that it's an assertion we seem to be unable to prove or disprove.

I could also assert that "Barney the Dinosaur is God" and I could not prove or disprove its veracity. That would be "the religion of Barney"—not "the science of."

Here's another famous what the baloney assertion also repeated by many popular self-help authors and metaphysicians:

> "Your mind can't tell the difference between what it sees and what it remembers."

This notion is put forth authoritatively in the film by Dr. Joseph Dispenza.

Doctor of . . . ?

Chiropractic.

Hardly makes him an authority of psychobiology, but let's give him a chance.

Dr. Dispenza presents a few positron-emission tomography (PET) scans as "proof" that the brain can not make the distinction between the remembered and the observed.

He accurately points out that the same area of the brain lights up when you remember something you observed.

Hallelujah, free at last!?

Not so fast . . .

Aside from the glaring fact that this evidence alone is most certainly not irrefutable proof of this theory, there is something else it ignores: glaring evidence to the contrary.

That is, other PET scans have also shown that the brain most clearly behaves differently when seeing and remembering. For example, things observed light up more brightly than things remembered on PET scans.

We could go on, but it's not necessary. Just be aware that what is presented as "irrefutable" in *What the Bleep!?* is most certainly not.

Like all pseudoscience this film gives the appearance of science, that is it presents some of the outward trappings of science, but ultimately it relies on authority and faith.

If someone asks you to accept something on faith, or on their authority, it's no longer science—it's influence.

It generates *belief* rather than flexible, truly scientific thinking.

Hey, what's wrong with that, Mark? Maybe the act of believing has some effect on reality.

That's true.

But it doesn't make Ramtha and her merry band of followers right, either.

Who knows, maybe belief does affect reality, maybe it doesn't.

Maybe it does to a certain extent, but to *what* extent?

Let's take a short detour and find out. . . .

The Curative Power of Belief

Again, you could use the "you must believe" line about anything.

I could sell you a rock from my backyard and say, "This is a magic rock; it will make you happy, but you must believe in its power for it to work." (Sorry, I ran out of wood chips.) And to a certain extent, if you believe it works, it *might* just have some effect.

At least as far back as 1785, scientists have known of a curious phenomenon called:

The placebo effect (Latin: *I shall please*.) The sometimes curative effect of an otherwise inert treatment which is dependent upon the recipient's faith that it will work.

This was a profound discovery!

What does this mean? That an inert substance can have a positive effect on the body if you believe it will?

Yep, that's exactly what that means. In fact, it's so widely accepted as fact that when preparing scientific studies for medicines, the use of double-blind methods must be employed to rule out the placebo effect.

A little-known corollary to this is:

The nocebo effect (Latin: *I shall harm*.) The presence of undesirable reactions to treatments thought to be caused by the patient's expectation of a negative result.

In the case of Dave, it's altogether possible that the improvement in his condition associated with the DUHP Chip in the beginning could have been the placebo effect.

Maybe it was; maybe it wasn't. It's saying that we know for sure, when we really don't, that gets us into trouble.

Now, this whole placebo business is quite funny for two reasons.

First, many people who *believe* in skepticism with a religious fervor will immediately dismiss any type of new or unusual treatment without sufficient analysis or rational discussion. "Are you stupid? That's obviously just the placebo effect!"

They go back to sipping their lattes feeling smug about their intellectual prowess.

But that's not science either; that, too, is faith.

Why?

Well, they are making that judgment without any real basis other than their faith that "all things that don't have the seal of approval from scientific figures I trust are bunk."

End of discussion.

(Interesting how pseudoscience takes many forms, isn't it? The fanatical skeptics are "true believers" of another sort—the kind who hate "true believers" of the stuff they don't believe in. Sort of like branding any "freedom fighter who isn't on my side" instantly as a "terrorist" whether they use terrorist tactics or not.)

The other irony is that those who are in the "belief cures" camp could actually be doing some profoundly important work here.

And that is . . .

The Real Insult of Pseudoscience

Rather than preaching "the value of belief" dogmatically from on high, these guys could be actually analyzing and deconstructing the placebo effect.

How does it work?

Can we call it up on tap?

Is there a way to intensify it?

That would be useful science—if studied in a flexible and rational way. (It probably wouldn't sell many "faith heals" home study courses, though.)

Both the skeptics and the believers are doing a real disservice to people by not teaching them how to find real answers to these questions themselves.

There are a few people out there who actually are asking these "kooky" questions in a genuinely scientific way.

Rupert Sheldrake, in my opinion, is one of them. Sheldrake has asked some rather odd questions and the answers are at times profound.

For example, he once asked if the "sense of being stared at" was real and measurable.

We all "have a feeling" that this exists. Does it?

In his film *7 Experiments to Change the World* Sheldrake shows how he performed an experiment to see if it can be measured and how you can do the same yourself quite easily.

As presented, it's fairly convincing that the phenomenon exists and is indeed measurable.

After studying this and other similar phenomena (how some pets know when their owners are coming home, how some pets have been known to return home from thousands of miles away), he has formulated a theory to describe it all: "morphic resonance."

Maybe it exists. Maybe it doesn't. What makes Sheldrake exceptional is that he's both examining it openly as a scientist (he sees it as a model that may or may not be valid) and asking a rather profound question.

A brave one, too.

Many traditional scientists would dismiss these notions as "nonsense" and "unworthy" of scientific research.

I tend to think that's probably not their inner scientist talking, but their fear of professional ostracism.

Groupthink.

Stupidity Training

The conversation between a True Believer and a True Skeptic isn't much of a conversation, really.

What you have are two people who are dead-set in their opinions ready to say just about anything to justify those opinions.

It's not an exploration of ideas, but a chest-pounding shouting match.

He who can yell the loudest and use the cleverest persuasive linguistic tricks wins.

When people talk this way and it's presented as "intelligent conversation" it trains people to think that's what intelligent conversation is supposed to sound like.

If they haven't seen an actual egoless intelligent conversation between people who are actually looking for the truth, they won't know any better.

This same pseudo-intelligent conversation takes place on most of the news "debate" shows as well.

Stupidity Training is freely available today.

That, in fact, is what Sheldrake, like many other scientists in the past, has experienced. Some scientists dismiss his work (I believe unfairly) as pseudoscience completely.

Now, I'm not knocking every person out there who ever tried rubbing two crystals together to see if a dollar bill would pop out of their third eye.

I'm also certainly not knocking anyone's faith.

I'm just saying: Evaluate the feedback like a scientist!

> That is to say: *honestly*. Without allowing your belief to skew your results.
>
> If it works—great. If not—try something else.
>
> Be honest.
>
> If it is your faith—accept that.
>
> Know the difference.

Remember that science doesn't require faith—only observation.

And be aware that when you put your faith in something, you have given up a little bit (or maybe a lot) of your control.

The alternative is, well, insanity—and there's a whole lot of that for sale today.

Ultimately, the problem with pseudoscience is that it forms more Invisible Walls in your mind.

It does so by sneaking into your mind through the loopholes of authority and then plants a trojan horse of potentially false information.

The purveyors of pseudoscience do this in order to gain some control over you, usually in order to sell you a product or get you to join their cult (and, by the way, cults are usually just sophisticated vehicles for selling and advertising products).

This same process is performed a bit more deliberately by governments and corporations. In that case it's called . . .

Disinformation

Combine influence and deliberate deception and what do you get?

Disinformation.

This is yet another Invisible Wall that is so pervasive that it deserves its own book.

Several even.

Why is it so popular?

Let's dig.

Political leaders throughout history have demonstrated a deep understanding of the power of a mental model. If you control a person's mental model, you control the person.

This practice is alive and well today.

"Perception management" was a term coined by the U.S. Army to describe the process of "massaging" information in order to support a particular aim.

This may sound like new high-tech mind control, but it's nothing new at all, really.

In the sixth century B.C. *The Art of War* by Sun Tzu advises:

> It is through the information brought by the converted spy that we are able to acquire and employ local and inward spies. It is owing to his information, again, that we can cause the doomed spy to carry false tidings to the enemy.

Then in the fifth century A.D. the mysterious "36 Stratagems" surfaced. No one knows who wrote them, but they are studied commonly in China to this day. Essentially they are simply 36 ways to hide your intentions from "the enemy."

We move on to the fifteenth century A.D. and Machiavelli's *The Prince* surfaces as a political guidebook for deceiving your public, your enemies, and your peers.

And not much has changed up to today. The act of deceiving both your public and your enemies is still alive and quite well.

Now, one might argue that the public doesn't have time to understand the deeper complexities of every political decision and every nuance of *realpolitik*, so a bit of perception management is okay. Necessary even.

Maybe so. but it may be a slippery slope. (And this statement may be a logical fallacy, by the way; I'll let you look it up and be the judge.)

Once you have given information a gentle massage with the best of intentions, what's next?

If we're going to massage the information a little, why not massage it a lot?

Hey, it's all in the name of the public interest, right?

The extreme of this is:

> **Disinformation** The act of deliberately spreading false information for an intended effect.

> "Uh-oh. Joyner isn't one of these anti-government whack-jobs, is he?"

Let's find out.

Before you go dismissing me as a conspiracy nut, do a bit of research. I don't know who you are, or where you're from, but chances are your government has in fact deliberately lied to you in the past, has been caught, and will probably do so again.

If you live in the United States, and you're a Democrat, you probably strongly suspect that the Republicans have lied to you in the past. If you're a Republican, you probably have the same suspicions of the Democrats.

In fact, you're probably *sure* of it.

Hint: You're right. Leaders from both of the dominant political parties in America have been caught red-handed telling the most outrageous lies to the American public. And some of our "allies" have been caught deceiving us as well. Instances of these can be found in even the most rigorous history books—not just the conspiracy pages. (I'll leave out any specific examples to avoid ruffling any partisan feathers. Do the research yourself from various sources.)

If you live outside the United States, before you go off on a smug see-how-messed-up-America-is-God-bless-*my*-country rant, know that your government has, too.

It should be noted that while we're quite sensitive to disinformation used against us when it is employed by "the enemy" (the enemy being anyone not on "your side"), we're likely to miss it when it's used in support of things we believe.

But wait, how can I really say all this?

I mean, what is a lie really? By saying this am I not making an assumption of someone else's motives? How can I possibly know?

Now you're thinking.

I *can't.*

While we do know in fact that political leaders have uttered falsehoods, we can't know that they did so deliberately.

Maybe it was an innocent mistake.

It would be almost impossible to know the motive or true intention of a specific politician (without a tremendous amount of damning evidence), but the existence of many books like *The Art of War* and *The Prince* would indicate that the practice does exist.

Not enough evidence?

How about this:

> Israel's version of the CIA, Mossad, even at one time used the motto: "By way of deception thou shalt do war."

At least, that's what former Mossad agent Victor Ostrovsky says. After the printing of his book *By Way of Deception* (1991) the government of Israel tried to stop the sale of the book in the United States and found it important enough to clarify that the book's title was a mistranslation of Mossad's "old" secret motto.

By the way, that was the first time in history a sovereign state attempted to stop the sale of a book in another sovereign state. Luckily it failed.

Why do I say "luckily"?

Well, I have no way of knowing whether what Ostrovsky says is true, but regardless I'm quite glad that the freedom of the press is strong enough in the United States to have prevented it from being subverted.

121

Chapter 8: Disinformation

(At least it was in that case. It may not be now.)

So maybe all of this is in fact conspiratorial madness.

Interestingly, depending on who's writing the history, accounts of events from around the globe vary widely.

History books in your own country are unlikely to have as scathing an account of your own country's past wrongs as, say, the version of events as told in unfriendly countries.

"But of course *they* would lie about us! They're biased!"

Guess what: *They* are saying the same thing about *you*.

If you are an American, you are probably quite familiar with the stories of Adolph Hitler falsifying an attack on Poland as a pretext for his invasion.

We recount this as fact and tend to accept it as so.

Let's see if you're as willing to accept the following tale of disinformation as readily:

> The Gulf of Tonkin incident is generally recognized as the event that provoked the Vietnam War. According to the standard telling of the story, U.S. Navy destroyers were attacked by Vietcong PT boats on August 4, 1964.

See, "they" started it.

Did they?

Admiral James Stockdale, who was then a pilot flying over the Gulf during the incident said (in the 1984 book he wrote called *In Love and War*), "[I] had the best seat in the house to watch that event, and our destroyers were just shooting at phantom targets—there were no PT boats there. . . . There was nothing there but black water and American firepower."

He recognizes that there was a legitimate and verifiable attack on August 2, 1964, but that the "attack" on August 4 was as he described.

Maybe it doesn't matter. Hey, they attacked us on the 2nd, right? What's wrong with lying about another attack?

Well, if we were indeed justified, why would we need to lie at all?

According to the *Pentagon Papers* not only was the government aware of Stockdale's observations, but ordered him to keep quiet.

The *Pentagon Papers?*

Oh, that's a 7,000-page top secret document. It was commissioned by Secretary of Defense Robert MacNamara and was never supposed to see the public light of day.

The official title is *United States-Vietnam Relations, 1945–1967: A Study Prepared by the Department of Defense* and it made fairly clear that the Johnson administration had deliberately expanded its role in Vietnam—it wasn't a matter of us being "provoked."

The document was leaked to the *New York Times* by former State Department employee Daniel Ellsberg.

Chances are, depending on where you live, you may remember a few other cases of disinformation on account of "the enemy."

Chapter 8: Disinformation

In your country, it may be acceptable, even downright patri-otic, to recount them.

If you were to bring up cases of disinformation perpetrated by your own country, you're likely to be dismissed as unpa-triotic and possibly a conspiracy nut.

Indeed, some Americans reading this might find it irrespon-sible to even suggest any of it.

Hmm. . . . Is it?

Since perception is everything, maybe information *should* be controlled. And maybe hacks like me should keep their mouths shut if we know a little dirty laundry.

Whose Side is Mark On?

Despite what you just read, my predisposition is to side with the United States. Perhaps it's *because* I am an American. My past as a U.S. Army officer and an agent (and even Distinguished Member) of the Military Intelligence Corps may make me even more predisposed to do so.

The *idea* of my country, though, is that it should be under "constant revolution." That is, the control is constantly shifting among various groups and interests. The system, as it is intended, is meant to keep any one person or group of people from having too much control.

It's believed that this protects the people.

Further, the appearance of constant revolution will prevent the people from becoming unhappy. It gives them a greater sense of control (something that was probably lacking in the regimes of Mao and Stalin).

It's not a bad idea. Maybe even one of the best ideas ever.

But belief in its utility doesn't preclude one from at times suspecting the intentions of the various holders of these offices and even holding them to task.

It also doesn't mean that the people in power at any given moment are infallible—and even at times influenceable by outside interests (including and not limited to: corporations, banking institutions, interest groups, and even foreign governments).

Chapter 8: Disinformation

One might argue that McNamara and Johnson saw a bigger picture. They believed that "the threat of communism" had to be "contained" and that Vietnam was an essential arena of containment.

Yeah.

The fact is, it's fairly clear that the greatest evils in history *did* occur while communist leadership was on watch.

God forbid it spreads to the rest of the world.

A small war and a few lies to prevent the spread of an evil responsible for the untimely deaths of more than 100,000,000 people may not be such a bad price to pay.

"Desperate times require desperate measures," right?

To fight "the enemy" we must do everything we can, even if it means deceiving the public for their own good.

Right?

That proposition may *or may not* be valid.

On the surface the justification is logical. Many communists did in fact believe that for communism to work, "the fight" had to be global.

That's a pretty scary thought.

I certainly am glad I'm a U.S. citizen and was not born under the regimes of Mao or Stalin.

My point isn't to argue this one way or the other, though.

The point is, the practice of disinformation is likely alive and well.

Any action, even murder, can be justified with context.

If you are given a fake context, you can be tricked into doing almost anything.

The extreme power of this is so seductive that even corporations are known to be actively involved in aggressive disinformation campaigns.

There are even companies you can hire who will go out to Internet bulletin boards and spread "positive lies" about you and defamatory lies about your competitors.

Hey, if the world believed that your competitor's products caused cancer, it could sure have an impact on their sales.

Chapter 8: Disinformation

Book II: The Invisible Walls

You can imagine the justifications given in the boardrooms:

> "Hey, their products *are* inferior. By speeding up their demise, we are doing the public a service."

Of course this is generally perceived as a deeply unethical and sleazy tactic, but it's common.

Corporate disinformation is so rampant on the net that a document titled *Twenty-Five Ways to Suppress the Truth: the Rules of Disinformation* is commonly disseminated on Web bulletin boards to help people spot corporate "shills." The author of these rules informs me that they have been downloaded more than 2,000,000 times and have appeared in political science, journalism, and psychology courses at many universities around the world. Here they are.

Twenty-Five Rules of Disinformation

From H. Michael Sweeney, author of *The Professional Paranoid* and other books on personal privacy and security. The original list can be found at http://www.proparanoid.net/truth.htm, and is also found in *The Professional Paranoid Defensive Field Guide* (ProParanoid Press, http://www.proparanoidpress.com). At the ProParanoid Press Web site, you can also find the *Alice in Amerikaland* music album which features a song about the 25 Rules. (I haven't heard the music album or read the book yet, I just find the rules useful.)

(Continued)

1. Hear no evil, see no evil, speak no evil.

2. Become incredulous and indignant.

3. Create rumormongers.

4. Use a straw man.

5. Sidetrack opponents with name-calling, ridicule.

6. Hit and run.

7. Question motives.

8. Invoke authority.

9. Play dumb.

10. Associate opponent charges with old news.

11. Establish and rely upon fall-back positions.

12. Enigmas have no solution.

13. Use Alice in Wonderland logic.

14. Demand complete solutions.

15. Fit the facts to alternative conclusions.

16. Vanish evidence and witnesses.

17. Change the subject.

18. Emotionalize, antagonize, and goad.

19. Ignore facts, demand impossible proofs.

20. False evidence.

21. Call a grand jury, special prosecutor.

22. Manufacture a new truth.

23. Create bigger distractions.

24. Silence critics.

25. Vanish.

Eight Traits of The Disinformationalist

1. Avoidance.

2. Selectivity.

3. Coincidental.

4. Teamwork.

5. Anticonspiratorial.

6. Artificial emotions.

7. Inconsistency.

8. Newly discovered: time constant.

So, as we have seen many people are manipulating your Invisible Walls—sometimes with the best of intentions—sometimes not:

There are the pseudoscientists and charlatans.

There are the political forces both friendly and enemy.

There are the business owners and friends.

Oh, and then there's . . .

You.

Book II: The Invisible Walls

Focus

Even if we have healthy beliefs about the world and about ourselves, they may not be enough to tear down the Invisible Walls completely.

Everything else in the world could be going for you, but if your focus is diverted away from this fact, it won't matter.

It's an amazing phenomenon. Someone could be fabulously rich, but if they choose to focus on "the suffering of the world" or "the injustice of it all" or "the futility of living," they can make themselves fabulously unhappy as well.

Hamlet comes to mind:

> Here was a prince born to great fortune, but "Something is rotten in the state of Denmark."

In theatre it is generally recognized that there are two types of serious dramatic plays: tragedy and melodrama.

Shakespeare categorized his plays as either tragedies, histories, or comedies, but modern critics would divide his tragedies into these two categories.

Melodrama is a situation that is unavoidable despite the best efforts of the victim of the events.

A *tragedy* is a play that describes unfortunate events as a result of a flaw in someone's character.

Now, it's interesting to note that (despite its being often referred erroneously to as "The Tragedy of Romeo and Juliet") most modern dramatic scholars now recognize *Romeo and Juliet* as a melodrama and not a tragedy.

Hamlet, however, was aptly named a tragedy.

To the untrained eye, one would say "but his father was assassinated and there was such treachery afoot! Therefore, it's a melodrama."

Indeed, but most seem to argue that it wasn't these events per se that led to his downfall, but the way he chose to react to them, hence revealing the character flaw that ultimately makes the play a tragedy.

Throughout the play (which if you haven't read 10 times you have stolen from yourself one of the great joys of art), Hamlet is obsessed with death and even considers killing himself (rather than taking action to make things right and change his world).

This, of course, is up for debate. The "real" motivation of Hamlet is a matter of opinion and his character is perhaps the most complex you'll ever find.

(An interesting exercise would be to read *Hamlet* several times and see how many of the Invisible Walls are affecting him.)

Another common interpretation of Hamlet's motivation is indecision.

It could be argued his inability to pick a single course of action drove him to depression.

And perhaps this is one of the reasons why we are wired for limited focus.

If we use the brain as computer model again, we might find that unlimited simultaneous access to all of your memory could overload your CPU.

The Russian journalist Solomon V. Shereshevskii, often referred to as "S" in psychological literature was reported to have had a near perfect (or "eidetic") memory. It's reported that he could remember the minutest details of events that had occurred years before.

In his earlier life he reported that the phenomenon produced "distractions." Common experiences could bring back a flood of seemingly unrelated experiences and over-whelm him.

This got worse throughout life and he ended up in an asylum. Conversations that occurred minutes before could not be distinguished in his mind from those that had occurred in years past.

So, perhaps these hardwired limitations are a blessing.

What do we know of these mechanisms?

Not much, but we have a few clues.

> As we learned from the Magic Number 7, there seems to be an upper limit to the *number* of things we can hold in our conscious attention at any given time.

> We also know that what we choose to consciously focus on seems to have an effect on what we see, as well.

If you've ever purchased a car, you may have "noticed" the same car popping up more frequently than before.

Those who believe in the metaphysical principle of the law of attraction would have you believe that you are thus "attracting" the car into your life because you focus on it.

(It's an interesting theory—often backed up authoritatively by What-the-Bleep-style pseudoscience. I have no problem with the belief in this "law" per se, as long as it's not passed off as dogma or science. One of my closest friends, Dr. Joe Vitale, is a firm proponent of the "law of attraction" but anyone who knows him will confirm that he's not dogmatic about this belief—or anything else for that matter. He's actually one of the most flexible and open people I know.)

Another explanation that may hold up more reliably to scientific scrutiny is that your "reticular activating system" is serving as a filter for information that enters your brain.

Somehow we're "selecting" the information that enters our brain and to a certain extent this is a controllable phenomenon.

How? Through conscious focus.

Whatever it is, it's a phenomenon that is readily observable.

(If you've finished *simple•*ology 101 by now you'll remember a do-at-home exercise that allows you to easily observe this phenomenon for yourself.)

We can manipulate this phenomenon for varying positive and negative effects.

Jakow Trachtenberg was a mathematician you might call "unlucky." He fled Russia after the revolution in 1917 because he saw that the government was tipping toward extremism.

To escape the madness he went to Germany. He was an outspoken critic of Hitler and a pacifist and eventually became a marked man, so he fled to Vienna. After the annexation of Austria in 1938 Trachtenberg was captured and sent to a concentration camp.

To take his mind off his imprisonment, he focused his attention inward and played with mathematics in his head. This was so effective at taking his mind off his surroundings that he left the camp after seven years with relatively little psychological scarring.

During that time he also developed, all in his head, a complete system of "speed math" widely known now as the Trachtenberg system.

It's amazing stuff. It allows otherwise normal people to calculate complex multiplication problems in their head without any paper or notes.

It's also a huge testament to the power of focus.

It's safe to say that those under similar circumstances who focused on the hopelessness of their situations had wildly different experiences—and may have even remembered things quite differently.

But sometimes our attention is diverted in unconscious ways as well. To understand this phenomenon it might be useful to take a look at . . .

Trances

Hypnotic trance is something about which we know very little.

Many will dismiss trance as pseudoscience, but the results of some clinical psychologists using hypnotherapy (most notably Milton Erickson) are well-documented and border on legendary.

The bad rap that hypnosis has is probably largely due to the number of lay practitioners around the world who put up a shingle and tout their methods as "miracle cures."

One theory of hypnotic trance purports that it can be induced by a manipulation of focused attention.

Milton Erickson was famous for his "handshake induction." With this technique, he would slightly alter his handshake by lingering just a little longer than expected. This unexpected

Heretics and Scientific Conservatism

Milton Erickson was largely against the use of hypnosis outside of a certified clinical setting (performed by a licensed clinical psychologist, not a graduate of a six-week course), and it's now easy to understand why. He was afraid of the tool being abused, and we can see now that it clearly has been. Such fears are the usual motivation for extreme conservatism in science.

Many otherwise imaginative men like Isaac Asimov and Carl Sagan (perhaps two of the most important men of the twentieth century) were extreme skeptics. Both were members of the group known as the Committee for the Scientific Inquiry of Claims of the Paranormal (CSICOP).

Some might argue that CSICOP members are dogmatically predisposed to disbelief in anything outside of the bounds of mainstream science. This could potentially close them off to being open to the works of people like Rupert Sheldrake.

I personally feel that Dr. Sheldrake's work has certainly been treated unfairly on the whole. He's far from a "fringe lunatic."

A fascinating exchange can be seen between Dr. Sheldrake and members of CSICOP here

In response to an experiment of Dr. Sheldrake's:
http://www.csicop.org/si/2000-09/staring.html

Dr. Sheldrake's reply:
http://www.csicop.org/si/2001-03/stare.html

The response from CSICOP:
http://www.csicop.org/si/2001-03/stare-reply.html

The last word?

The last word is granted to CSICOP but here's a link to Dr. Sheldrake's web site where you can even participate in live online experiments to check things out for yourself: http://www.sheldrake.org

Sheldrake reports that CSICOP was in fact able to reproduce some of Sheldrake's experiments on "the sense of being stared at" so I wouldn't dismiss this man as a crack-pot offhand.

I must admit, I'm a "fan" of Dr. Sheldrake, and I don't think this requires an apology. He's amazingly brave to ask these questions and persist despite the criticism of some of his peers.

It's thinking and bravery like his that propels science forward. Louis Pasteur comes to mind.

However, I'm also a fan of Drs. Asimov and Sagan, sadly both now long past. It's possible that the CSICOP organization has morphed a bit from what it was when they were alive.

Asimov argued that there was value in extreme skepticism. He saw the body of knowledge as being "under attack" by pseudoscience and quackery, and he was quite right!

This attack reaches even higher levels of intensity as the media through which we spread information become more common and speedy.

Asimov recognized that it is indeed the heretic that often propels science forward in radical leaps. But he also rightfully pointed out that such heretics were rare in comparison to the insane heretic spouting nonsense.

(Continued)

141

Chapter 10: Trances

As such, CSICOP sees itself as a righteous defender of the revered body of scientific knowledge.

In some sense, that's a useful notion, but once we start dismissing things offhand as pseudoscience without any examination (and base our judgments solely on our existing model of the world), we ourselves have left the bounds of the scientific and have entered the realm of the true believer.

Sheldrake's account of his interaction with the famous skeptic "The Amazing Randi" demonstrates this beautifully: http://www.sheldrake.org/D&C/controversies/randi.html

A great counterpoint is Asimov's famous essay about "Endoheretics" and "Exoheretics."

action was theorized to "disrupt" the thought flow of the recipient just long enough to give an "entry" into their mind. At that point, a hypnotic suggestion can be given and a trance induced.

This is what is commonly referred to as a "pattern interrupt." It's used in various therapeutic settings to disrupt someone's consciousness in order to leverage change.

In a sense, hypnosis is about interrupting, manipulating, or shutting off the conscious process of thinking and awareness, thus allowing information to pass into your mind unchallenged.

While Erickson's handshake induction may sound a little spooky, many claim that it works surprisingly well.

So is hypnotic trance uncommon? Maybe not.

It has been argued that the process of watching television is hypnotic and that the trancelike state of the viewer makes them extremely susceptible to persuasion (be it from the politician giving a speech or the commercial selling them salvation).

Some people are so skilled at speech that just listening to them speak can have a hypnotic effect.

We even put ourselves into trances from time to time. My favorite is what I call the "I-already-know-that trance." You can observe this in yourself when every time someone gives you some good advice, you say, "I already know that," and then fail to act on it.

It might even be argued that we are all under one form of trance or another in every waking moment. That is, in order to hold our current model of the world in mind, and use it to effectively navigate our surroundings, we have to enter into a state that could be called a trance.

So, what *trance* are you in right now?

Perhaps some of them are caused by your . . .

Runaway Brainware

Yet another Invisible Wall may take the form of mental "programs" run amuck in our brains.

If you own a computer, you've probably noticed that when you have too many windows open, your computer gets sluggish. Closing those windows down (unless the program running was poorly programmed with a "memory leak") will generally bring the computer back up to a healthy running pace.

You can notice this phenomenon in yourself whenever you get overwhelmed or "overstimulated." It's like you have too many programs running and your RAM and CPU can't keep up.

The problem is that sometimes we don't notice this programming. It's running in the background.

If your computer has ever been infected by a virus or uninvited "adware," you might see the slowdown but not know why.

The same thing can be observed in our own minds.

Have you ever felt weighed down by past problems looming in your memory? (This is why "closure" on a past issue always feels so good.)

Or maybe you have a million things to do piling up and it's almost like

> ". . . . loose ends, tying a noose in the back of my mind."
>
> —Beck

This "runaway brainware" is quite common but can be handled in the same way as hidden runaway programs on your computer; you identify them and you shut them down.

If you've been using your free *simple•*ology WebCockpit software, we have tools built in there that, among other things, help you get more "processing power" out of your brain by shutting down your runaway brainware. It's actually really easy and takes only 15 minutes a day.

And it may help you to take better advantage of your . . .

Chapter 11: Runaway Brainware

Neural Networking

To a certain extent we can observe that as our model of the world changes, the "wiring" in our head changes as well.

Again, among our very limited knowledge of how the brain actually works, we do know that the brain is composed of billions of neurons and that the connections between these neurons are in a constant state of flux.

As we form new memories and associations in our mind, parallel connections in our brain are formed as the neurons adapt and connect to each other.

This "neural networking" has been mimicked in the most advanced computer systems to make our computers even closer in operation to the human brain.

Why is this important?

Well, it seems that these connections are not always perfectly "rational" ones. Without any control or apparent order to these connections, the results can be unpredictable.

For example, if a traumatic event happens to you and there is a distinctive odor present, the event and the odor are now "linked up" in your brain. Being exposed to that smell could "trigger" a memory of that event and even thrust you into depression.

This phenomenon (smells triggering memories) are referred to in psychology as "Proustian memories" (from the novel *Remembrance of Things Past* by Marcel Proust). Psychological literature is chock-full of reported cases of it.

While this is a very specific phenomenon that almost everyone has observed from their personal experience ("Where do I know that smell? It reminds me of . . . "), it's possible that this is only the tip of the iceberg and that the effects are more far reaching and subtle than we realize.

While we can only consciously focus on the Magic 7 items at any one time, our brain is actually taking in quite a bit more information in every moment.

It is believed that the strength of a memory is greatly enhanced by focused attention (which is why active engagement is so crucial for effective learning), so the information we are taking in unconsciously is likely not to have as deep an impression.

However, it is still there and it can affect us in unpredictable ways (*a la* the cases of a smell from long ago triggering an onset of depression).

What's frightening about this is that these connections are occurring constantly in the background, and it is not possible for us to control them completely.

In fact, it's likely that the vast majority of the connections we make in our mind happen unconsciously.

And it's not just smell that can affect us. With every experience we are simultaneously taking in a massive volume of "additional information" that is being "linked up" as we go along.

It's happening in your mind right now.

It doesn't take a smell to trigger one of these connections. They can be triggered by virtually anything.

It can even be something far more subtle than the connections of thoughts with senses.

Going back to Dave.

When he was a young man, he had great respect for his mother. Anything she said was like the word of God.

Dave's mom was an artist and an entrepreneur. She never worked a day in her life.

One morning they were having breakfast watching the TV news. The story was about an employee at the local Wal-Mart being selected as the Employee of the Month because he took the initiative to drive a seventy-year-old woman, who had a flat tire, home.

DAVE'S MOM

Ha!

DAVE

What's so funny?

DAVE'S MOM

Employee of the Month.

DAVE

Is that bad?

DAVE'S MOM

Honey, full-time jobs are for suckers.

From that point forward, he always associates the idea of a full-time job with distaste and hated every job he's ever had.

Notice how many of the influence and linguistic factors you learned are at play here?

Well, not only can they influence us to change our opinions and our behavior in the moment, but if the neural networking is strong enough, they can affect us our entire lives.

So, is it all doom and gloom for us?

Is there hope for humanity?

Well, that remains to be seen (at the time of writing we have not blown ourselves up yet), but history has thrown us a few life-lines.

Some mighty powerful lifelines, indeed. Read on.

Book I:
The Asylum

Why you're stuck where you are now.

Book II:
The Invisible Walls

Your defective mental hardware and other programming anomalies that prevent you from getting what you want.

Offensive weapons used against you to keep you there.

Book III:
Disposable Reality

A new Operating System for the brain.

Defensive weapons to break your way out.

You are here.

Book IV:
simple•ology

The Simple Science of Getting What You Want

The Programming Language for writing programs that turn dreams into reality.

How to get to where you want to be.

Disposable Reality

Introduction

Being aware of the Invisible Walls is the first step in freeing yourself.

The next, and equally important, key is something I call Utilitarian Model Flexibility (UMF).

First, it seems we're now faced with a problem. Once we understand that any thought or idea we have is, by definition, going to be at least slightly flawed, it immediately unbinds us from that model.

So is that it? We just unbind ourselves from our model and we're free, right?

Not exactly.

In order for us to function in the world, we have to accept the validity of a particular model—at least for a moment. Without this, decision making is impossible.

Think about it. Look around the space you're in right now. If you can't trust that any of it is real, is it safe to even move around?

So, which option do we take:

- Accept a rigid faulty model and allow it to control us.
- Accept nothing at all and live in paralysis.

It seems like a double bind, and it is.

Do you remember the solution? The key to solving a double bind is to remember that there is always another option.

We don't choose between those two options. We choose *neither.*

The option that seems to give us the most freedom and simultaneously the most power is what I call the Utilitarian Model Flexibility model.

It works like this. For whatever reason in any given moment in time, you may have certain wants, needs, or desires.

In order to get those things (serving some purpose—that is, some utility), we try various things. Some of these things work. Some don't.

Based on what we want in any given moment, we are flexible with our model and adopt one that serves whatever our utility is in that moment.

Utilitarian—serving some purpose or aim.

Model—your model of the world.

Flexibility—changeable at will.

So, you simply change your model of the world in ways that serve whatever your given aims are.

> *You aren't paralyzed by the futility in finding a perfect model.*
>
> *You aren't stuck in a rigid model that is eventually going to fail.*
>
> *You're flexible.*

Book III: Disposable Reality

If this sounds like a radically different way to live, you're right. It is. But you're already doing this to a certain extent right now.

For example, pick up an object close to you and drop it.

Isaac Newton's laws of motion and gravity can describe these actions quite accurately and quite predictably.

You have a model of the physical world that is largely based upon Newton's laws, and you expect them to be an accurate predictor of the way the world works.

Over time you begin to trust it. However, if you were attempting to predict the movement of "quantum" particles, this model would no longer be useful. If you attempted to describe the movement of these particles in this way, your model would fall apart.

So, you could adopt a newer model that more accurately describes the behavior of quantum particles.

That's what quantum physics is about despite the common misconception that *quantum* means "big." A "quanta" is actually just a *part* or a *particle*.

A less abstract example might best be illustrated this way:

> When I was in the U.S. Army I developed various models in my mind about leadership. Some of them were more effective than others (I was at various points in my career an excellent soldier and a terrible one).
>
> When I resigned my commission and entered the civilian world (almost becoming a Special Agent in the FBI, I

passed the rigorous selection process but ended up not entering—long story), I carried this model of leadership to my new business.

I was eventually able to see that at least some of what I "knew" about leadership simply did not apply to this new environment. The old model was now faulty.

The problem was that it took me time to let go of that model. Because of my past experience I developed a certain amount of "conviction"/rigidity about leadership.

Despite the problems it caused, I resisted change.

If I had at the time been consciously practicing the UMF model, I would not have been so stuck in the model that wasn't working.

It's exactly this lack of flexibility in our models that creates a tremendous amount of pain and suffering in our lives.

And knowing now that these models are not always formed by us consciously, we can see how vulnerable we are to the utility of others.

If someone else controls your model, it's no longer serving your purpose; it's serving theirs.

These examples are but two of many. Almost certainly you are carrying around a number of models in your head right now that are not serving any positive utility for you at all.

Sometimes letting these models go can be quite difficult—especially if they are fundamental to our identity (religious, cultural, political).

You may have the association in your mind that:

changing your mind = a bad thing

In fact, if you accept Cialdini's consistency model of influence, we may even be hardwired for inflexibility.

If we change our model, we may be afraid of people saying:

> "Well, aren't you the one who used to say that all Arabs were terrorists? What happened to that?"

Instead of being flexible and saying "that model may have been wrong" we have to justify ourselves:

> "Oh, well I *still* think they are all terrorists, and my new girlfriend may be Arab, but she hates Arabs, too."

We're masterful at concocting logical justifications for our desperate clinging to a rigid model—despite overwhelming evidence that it's no longer serving us!

UMF is a great tool, but its effectiveness can be greatly enhanced with a few conceptual skills.

To carry on with the brain as personal computer metaphor, these skills are like Operating System enhancements that allow your "machine" to run more efficiently.

Book III teaches you skills that will allow you to

- More accurately predict in advance if a model will work.
- Help identify faulty models without having to test them yourself.

- More accurately evaluate your judgments about the models you create.

- Help you to discover new models—and even invent new models out of thin air.

This is just a start for you. On these topics, too, you should become a lifelong student.

A Look Ahead

What if you could upgrade the other parts of your computer/brain? Is it possible?

You can easily upgrade the various elements of your actual personal computer by going to a local computer store, but such a store does not exist for the human brain.

simple•ology, the company we've invented around these ideas, is like the upgrade store for your brain.

The 3-Point simple •*ology Plan for Upgrading Your Brain*

1. *Upgrading your hardware.* Unfortunately, we can't just snap in a chip that will give you bigger and faster hard storage, processing power, or RAM, but we do know a few things about the brain that will gradually help you to "build" a more powerful brain.

   For example, we know that exercising the brain in certain ways and improving overall health can give your brain a literal hardware upgrade. We offer software and courses to help you do that (much of it is free).

You can also learn more about the inherent flaws and limitations built into your mental CPU and learn how to work around them for better processing (covered in Book II and in what you're about to read in Book III).

2. *Upgrading your operating system.* UMF is like your ultimate Operating System for the mind. Instead of having just one OS, it's like having an infinite number of OSs and allowing you to switch between them as needed.

   In the PC world, we have "dual boot" machines that can let you switch between Linux, Mac, or Windows (the three most popular PC OSs).

   UMF is an "infinite boot" machine—and you don't even have to "reboot"; you just switch at will.

3. *Upgrading your programming.* Once you have a useful model of the world, so what? Does it just mean you can now sit around in your local café, sip a latte, and enjoy your superior view of the world?

   It's unlikely this will get you what you want unless what you want is to sit around and feel smug all day, in which case, knock yourself out.

   Some programs are more effective than others.

   In Book IV (and in your free multimedia companion course *simple•ology* 101) you learn a new program that is extremely efficient in getting you from "wanting it" to "having it."

Logic

W_e all think we know what logic is, but scholars of logic will disagree as to its meaning. Philosophers of ancient Greece, India, and China all independently attempted to answer the question:

How do you evaluate the validity of the spoken word?

Or plainly:

How do you know whether what someone is saying is bullshit?

Sometimes we hear someone say something and on the surface it sounds right, but we just know "something is wrong" and we can't put our finger on it.

Logic attempts to put a finger squarely on what's *wrong* in such statements (a la the logical fallacies) and what makes other statements *right*.

In one sense, logic is a set of helpful rules that will allow you to know if a linguistic model, at least on the surface, is valid.

But what does that mean exactly?

Well, at its core, even though there are many different logical approaches, any argument can be evaluated in two ways:

Soundness   The "truth" of the underlying presuppositions ("statements") of an argument.

Validity   An argument's adherence to the laws of logic.

The definition for validity sounds circular, and it is. That circularity will make perfect sense in a moment.

Remember that when logisticians say "argument" they are not talking about two people fighting; they are simply referring to a collection of statements that are being presented as truth.

Depending on the various rules of logic you choose to accept, "validity" may vary.

To help you understand, here's an argument:

All Yorkshire terriers are dogs.

Rusty is a Yorkshire terrier.

Therefore, Rusty is a dog.

Each of those sentences are *statements*. Presented together they are an *argument*.

Let's look at soundness.

"All Yorkshire terriers are dogs."

Must people would accept that statement to be "true." So far, the argument is sound.

"Rusty is a Yorkshire terrier." Since Rusty is a hypothetical fantasy dog that lives in the same imaginary world as Dave we have no way of knowing whether this is true. For the sake of the argument, let's just say it's true.

We have a sound argument!

What about validity?

If you accept Aristotelian logic, this argument does in fact fall under Aristotle's various rules of the "syllogism."

The particular rule can be described as.

> All Ps are Q.
> X is a P.
> Therefore, X is a Q.

Here's another argument that looks dangerously similar to the preceding one, but is radically different:

> All Yorkshire terriers are dogs.
> Rusty is a dog.
> Therefore, Rusty is a Yorkshire terrier.

The first two statements are true, so the argument is sound.

The conclusion, however, is fallacious or *invalid*.

Using Aristotle's model, we can see it's a corruption of the basic syllogism.

It does not necessarily follow that Rusty is a Yorkshire terrier if we accept the first two statements as true.

If you are practiced in the ways of syllogistic logic, you would be able to identify the bullshit of this statement quite readily.

If you're not studied in this way, it could throw you off. Without the proper time to evaluate things, you would simply be left confused (and your model of the world potentially corrupted with nonsense).

See how this helps you to select more useful models?

Now, it might seem that we have the keys to the universe here. Is logic an incorruptible set of rules that govern "the way things work?" Unfortunately it's not that simple.

Take this statement:

The car is a Ford.

It may very well be true.

What if we then say:

The car is a Ford. The same car is a Mitsubishi.

One of the laws of "classical logic" is the law of "bivalency."

That is, something is either true or false.

Yes, I mean it's crazy to think that it's a Ford *and* a Mitsubishi; it's one or the other.

This is where things get interesting:

What if the car was a collaborative effort of both Ford and Mitsubishi? Well, then it would be "true" but the law of bivalency no longer seems to hold up, does it?

Over time more complex forms of logic have been developed to describe exceptional relationships ("multivalued logic" and "fuzzy logic" for example).

In this case, a better way to describe it would be needed. It's part Ford and part Mitsubishi. Bivalence doesn't apply.

So as we can see here, even the laws of logic are subject to flexibility.

Even these new systems of logic may one day be improved upon.

As you can see now, the evaluation of an argument's validity is dependent upon your acceptance of particular logical rules.

While the type of logic we're talking about here describes the validity of verbal arguments, there are other logics that govern other relationships.

For example, other "logics" govern various branches of mathematics and computer programming.

All of these things are various types of *languages* and we agree to a set of rules that govern them. Sometimes the rules apply. Sometimes they don't.

Is Bivalence Dead Then?

An event that occurred while I was writing this book made me keenly aware of the utility of bivalence.

I walked out of my office to catch some air for a moment and went back, only to realize that I had locked my key inside. It was 10 P.M. so no one else was around. Despite a few various clever attempts to get back in, I was stuck outside.

I either had my key or I didn't. No tiny amount of fuzziness was going to save me. In this case, I most certainly did not have my key.

I took a cab home and luckily my fiancée was home and we had a spare. I had to compare the spare key to others to make sure it was the right one.

The spare was either right or it wasn't. There wasn't any other key that would "sort of" work. It would either work or it wouldn't.

So, just because a model of the world is newer, and even more accurate or useful in certain cases, doesn't mean we should chuck out the old one entirely.

Utility.

And these various languages are all just symbolic representations of the things we see and the things we think—they are not the things themselves.

It would really take a completely new text to give a better treatment of this topic, but I hope I've inspired you to take up the study of logic as an enhancement to your Operating System.

Now, once you have a solid grip on validity, how do you *really* determine an argument's soundness?

For example, if someone made the statement:

A force in motion always remains in motion.

Is it sound?

How do we know?

How, in general, can we know if an argument is sound?

What do we even *know* about the universe?

For thousands of years people have dedicated their lives to finding the answer to that question. They call this practice . . .

Science (Again)

While Logic is about the validity of arguments, science is ultimately about the soundness of statements.

If this sounds like a bivalent true/false statement, you are right.

As we know, bivalence is not always adequate in many cases, and this is certainly one of them.

Put another, perhaps more useful, way:

While logic provides a framework for the symbols we use to describe the world, science is a method of gathering a deeper understanding of our world through observation.

What do we mean by "deeper understanding?"

Well, science is really nothing more than a formal process of developing newer and more useful models of the world.

I propose that a "pure scientist" should have flexibility and be naturally opposed to rigidity by definition.

But as we know, scientists—human as they are—can at times be guilty of holding onto one model or another rigidly.

Sometimes scientists present statements as rigid capital-T Truth that is not to be questioned.

Of course, we're no longer scientists when we do this, but dogmatists, zealots, and charlatans. A scientist, by definition, should understand this relationship between the various models of the world and the world itself.

While a proper treatment of the ways of Science can hardly be given in a short chapter, here are a few useful concepts to get you started.

Science in the formal sense usually begins with . . .

Hypothesis

A *hypothesis* is a tentative "possible model" to explain a given "phenomenon" or "observable event."

For example, we may ask ourselves, Why do some men go bald?

Well, we might form the hypothesis that it is caused by eating cheeseburgers.

Hey, crazier things have been known to be true.

So, how would we "know" whether or not this hypothesis "held water?"

First, we'd need to learn a bit about . . .

Scientific Method

This is a step-by-step process for doing just that: testing to see if a hypothesized truth can be observed as reality.

The steps can be described in various ways, but in the most basic sense they are:

1. State a problem/question (Why is the sky blue? How can I increase my reading speed?).
2. Formulate a hypothesis.
3. Test the hypothesis.
4. Collect and analyze the data (what you observe during the test)
5. Draw a conclusion.

It has been stated many other ways, and there are several various methods of scientific inquiry—each of which with its own subtleties, but that's the core of it.

As you see, you can not only apply this to "model creation" but also to the solution of practical problems as well.

If we affirm our hypothesis through various forms of testing, we may eventually form a . . .

Theory

A *theory* is a more substantiated and detailed explanation for a particular set of phenomena that has some reliable predictive value.

For example, the theory of evolution is a possible explanation for how species came to be what they are.

Since it's up for debate and perhaps something we may never be able to know with a greater level of certainty, it's possible it may never become a . . .

Law

If a theory is tested and shown to be true by the general scientific community over a long period of time, it may be elevated to the status of a law.

The widely accepted laws of science are usually known for their simplicity and elegance. In fact, many of the laws of physics some would argue are absolute and irrefutable.

Of course, throughout the history of science, laws have at times been adjusted to account for new information.

Newton's laws of motion still hold true, but with the caveat now that they don't describe the behavior of quantum particles or of objects moving at extremely high speed.

So, even here flexibility is a requirement.

In fact, everything that we've just been talking about requires the inherent presupposition that things "are" and, well, maybe they're not.

Huh?

Yes, you should be confused. Read on for a lifeline.

E-Prime?

As you may remember from Book II, sometimes language gets in the way of our properly understanding the world.

The field of general semantics, pioneered by Alfred Korzybski in his seminal work "Science and Sanity," attempts to break down and analyze this relationship between language and reality.

Korzybski recognized that our defective mental model could potentially cause serious behavioral dysfunction and felt strongly that this was rooted in the inherent nature of our language.

While teaching a class on General Semantics, Dr. Korzybski once pulled a beautiful trick on his students.

He said that he was hungry and couldn't wait any longer to eat, so he pulled out a box of biscuits from his desk.

He started eating one and then offered some to his class.

After chewing on the biscuits and discussing how good they were, the good doctor pulled off the wrapper of the box to reveal that they were in fact dog biscuits.

The legend goes that a few of the students vomited on the spot.

It goes to show how our language defines our model and how our model defines our personal reality.

The students' experience of the biscuits was immediately changed by simply giving them a new label.

Korzybski felt that much of the problem was our inadequate and unhealthy use of the verb *to be*.

What did he mean?

Well, it would seem that if you say something *is*, you presuppose an absolute.

John is a fascist.

This statement does not allow for any shades of meaning. You either agree he is a fascist or you don't.

Remember the limitation of bivalent logic?

Simple "is" statements only make sense when you deal in absolutes. But it would seem that absolutes are rarely (if ever) adequate for describing the world.

An extreme interpretation of this theory (that may not be too far off the mark) would state that we're almost always creating a mild double bind when we use the words *to be*.

> John may exhibit some behaviors that some may interpret as "fascist."
>
> He may share some beliefs that are also shared by certain "fascist" ideologies.
>
> But he may also be (and likely is) one thousand other things that contradict this.
>
> *Is* John a fascist?

Even agreeing to such a statement in casual conversation is likely to set up a certain amount of cognitive dissonance if your knowledge of John goes beyond the trivial.

Now Korzybski never advocated the complete eradication of the verb to be from the English language, though some mistakenly believe he did.

What he called for was a recognition that *to be* could at times be replaced by more accurate language that might promote healthier thinking.

E-prime (English prime) was an invention of D. David Bourland after Korzybski's death. He proposed a modified version of English that eradicated the verb *to be* entirely in order to create more accurate models.

It's a fascinating concept!

Of *course*, in everyday life: E-prime *is* most impractical.

Or, in E-prime: *The people I have observed seem to find the use of E-prime impractical.*

If you talk like that all the time, things can get clumsy.

Kenneth Keyes Jr. proposed a more practical way to apply Korzybski's work to everyday life, known as The 6 Tools for Thinking. They are extremely useful and will instantly give you much greater clarity of thinking.

1. *So Far as I Know.*

   Adding this phrase to your language helps you identify that all knowledge is incomplete. If you say, *Bill Clinton is a pathological liar* you're making a statement based on limited information.

   "So far as I know Bill Clinton is a pathological liar" still perhaps isn't a rational deduction after watching him only on TV, but we're getting there (we all watched him lie once, but it doesn't mean his lying was a pattern—or anything else for that matter). At least we're now acknowledging the limits of our knowledge.

2. *Up to a Point.*

   As we learned earlier, most things are not simple "either/or" propositions. We don't live in a black/white world.

"So far as I know, Bill Clinton is a liar, up to a point."

Much better. Now we're no longer dealing in absolutes.

3. *To Me.*

Even if we recognize that our knowledge is limited and things are not absolute, we still must come to grips with the fact that our model predisposes us to judge things in a certain way.

Saying "to me" acknowledges that.

"To me, Bill Clinton is a genius."

4. *The What Index.*

Sometimes we make general statements about the world that fail to pay respect to the uniqueness of everything.

"Men are pigs."

Some women have been known to say that. Of course believing this binds the speaker to that particular model of reality and precludes them from alternatives.

For example, a woman believing this could meet the nonpiggy guy of her dreams, but if she believes that "men are pigs" she is likely to perceive him to be so and judge his actions accordingly.

NON-PIG

May I hold the door for you?

PIG BELIEVER

Why, so you can sleep with me and brag about it to your friends?

Man A may be a pig. But Man A is not Man B.

Or, as they would say in general semantics, Man_1 is not Man_2.

5. *The When Index.*

"Okay, so Man$_1$ is a pig, but maybe not all men are."

Progress.

But there's more.

As things are constantly changing in the world, it is important to value statements in regard to *when* they are true.

For example, Man$_1$ may have been a pig in 2005, but after some humbling and life-changing events he became pretty cool in 2006.

So, "Man$_1$ was a pig in 2005" is a more accurate statement (but still flawed as you can judge from the other tools).

6. *The Where Index.*

"Okay, in 2005 Man$_1$ was a real dirty rotten pig; we're all in agreement."

Not so fast.

It's possible that he acted like a pig only when he went to Miyagi's on Sunset Boulevard.

More accurate (but still perhaps unhealthy) would be:

"In 2005 every time I saw Man$_1$ at Miyagi's, he was a pig."

Applying these rules to your speech at the right times can unbind you from "*is*ness" and will do so without the clumsiness of E-prime.

Note: Perhaps I should say, "News commentators, politicians, and smart-ass writers." A casual reread of this book will likely reveal hundreds of examples of language that fail to live up to Keyes' standards. It may also demonstrate my own personal bias revealed in my choice of language. Good. Perhaps it will motivate you to stop putting complete trust in all authority figures including authors like me.

Now, if only we could teach this to our news commentators and politicians!

Even if you've mastered your language, there will still be times when you are faced with problems in your life not caused exclusively by language or your model.

It could be that you are driving out in the middle of nowhere and you run out of gas.

You could panic, you could rub your prayer beads together and hope the solution will manifest itself out of the quantum ether, or . . .

Polya

How is it that we actually solve *real* world problems?

There are infinite ways to answer that question of varying degrees of utility.

Perhaps the best was put forth by the Stanford University mathematician G. Polya.

It's an elegant and extremely useful method described in his now classic book *How to Solve It*—a highly recommended read.

This method can be applied to problems ranging from mathematics to the completely abstract.

As an exercise, imagine this problem (running out of gas in the middle of nowhere) and see if you can apply these steps to it.

Polya's 4-Step Problem Solving Method

Summary taken from G. Polya, *How to Solve It*, 2d ed., Princeton University Press, 1957, ISBN 0-691-08097-6.

1. Understanding the Problem

   - *First.* You have to understand the problem.

   - What is the unknown? What are the data? What is the condition?

   - Is it possible to satisfy the condition? Is the condition sufficient to determine the unknown? Or is it insufficient? Or redundant? Or contradictory?

   - Draw a figure. Introduce suitable notation.

   - Separate the various parts of the condition. Can you write them down?

2. Devising a Plan.

   - *Second.* Find the connection between the data and the unknown. You may be obliged to consider auxiliary problems if an immediate connection cannot be found. You should obtain eventually a plan of the solution.

   - Have you seen it before? Or have you seen the same problem in a slightly different form?

   - *Do you know a related problem? Do you know a theorem that could be useful?*

   - *Look at the unknown!* Try to think of a familiar problem having the same or a similar unknown.

- Here is a problem related to yours and solved before. Could you use it? Could you use its result? Could you use its method? Should you introduce some auxiliary element in order to make its use possible?

- Could you restate the problem? Could you restate it still differently? Go back to definitions.

- If you cannot solve the proposed problem try to solve first some related problem. Could you imagine a more accessible related problem? A more general problem? A more special problem? An analogous problem? Could you solve a part of the problem? Keep only a part of the condition, drop the other part; how far is the unknown then determined, how can it vary? Could you derive something useful from the data? Could you think of other data appropriate to determine the unknown? Could you change the unknown or data, or both if necessary, so that the new unknown and the new data are nearer to each other?

- Did you use all the data? Did you use the whole condition? Have you taken into account all essential notions involved in the problem?

3. Carrying Out the Plan

- Third. Carry out your plan.

- Carrying out your plan of the solution, check each step. Can you see clearly that the step is correct? Can you prove that it is correct?

(Continued)

4. Looking Back

- *Fourth. Examine* the solution obtained.

- Can you *check the result?* Can you check the argument?

- Can you derive the solution differently? Can you see it at a glance?

- Can you use the result, or the method, for some other problem?

As you can see, Polya's method is a deadly effective tool. You may also notice that it has some similarities to the scientific method.

Note: A useful addition to Step 1 might be to also ask, "Is it even really a problem?" Sometimes the answer is "no," but the Invisible Walls have caused us to believe it is so.

Chances are you have a few problems in your life right now. Whatever they are (from "I don't have a girlfriend" to "I can't sleep at night"), apply this method and the results may shock you.

Now, let's tie all this together with a few . . .

Rules for UMF

So, are you ready to put this new Operating System to work?

Here is an informal set of rules for applying Utilitarian Model Flexibility to your daily life.

Rule #1: Thoughts Are Not Things—Thoughts Are Models

Thought is anything you can hold in your mind—it is always a symbolic representation of something (either real or imaginary)—and never a thing in itself.

Beliefs, ideas, speech, are representations, incomplete and in flux.

It might be helpful to classify thoughts into two categories.

Representations of the Observed

Remember that even what we observe isn't the actual reality itself. What we see is actually a reconstructed representation of what we're looking at, and this representation is always incomplete and flawed.

But we create models of the observed in other ways as well—not just as pictures in our minds.

For example, you might look at something and then attempt to describe it verbally to someone else.

These words form a *verbal* model of the *visual* Model of the object you saw.

Notice that we've switched from one model to another in an attempt to describe the same thing.

As you can imagine, every time we go from model to model, and get further away from the original observation, the model is likely to become less and less accurate.

Try this:

> Look at a complex picture of a landscape.
>
> Attempt to describe the landscape to a friend and ask them to draw what you're describing.
>
> Then compare what they draw to the picture itself.
>
> Ask them if what they heard you say was the same as the picture they had drawn in their head.

You looked at the picture and created a model of it in your mind.

You then created a new verbal model of that picture and communicated it to your friend.

Your friend then created yet another model in their brain based on what you said.

They then attempted to communicate this with yet another model on paper.

Notice that each time we were talking about the same thing but that each model was probably wildly divergent.

What you just experienced was the day-to-day experience of normal communication.

It's no wonder we have conflict.

Even if we're on the same page with someone else conceptually, we may (and often do) fail in communicating it.

This gets even stickier when our thoughts are . . .

Representations of the Imaginary

These are beliefs, notions, theories, constructs.

Take for example *democracy:*

You can't feel it or touch it or sense it. It exists only as a collection of ideas and a general consensus of its meaning.

But try this:

> Ask your same friend now to write down a definition of democracy.
>
> Write one down yourself independently.
>
> Now compare the two.

What happened? Depending on who your friend is and their past experiences and beliefs, your definition could have been fairly close to theirs or wildly divergent.

Knowing this, it makes it all the more amusing when we watch pundits on television ranting and raving about . . .

The capital-T-Truth of this concept or that . . .

The wickedness or infalability of this group or that . . .

And then we watch on and nod in agreement or defy them—all the while not even agreeing or disagreeing about the same *thing*.

Note: To those who have the belief that "thoughts are things" (a notion that is taught by more than a few self-help gurus and metaphysicians—usually as irrefutable dogmatic capital-T Truth—by golly it's backed up by quantum physics and ten-thousand-year-old "channeled entities" far wiser than any of us—*obey!*) I challenge them to test the utility of that model. Also, see if you can reconcile it with the following (not-so-dogmatic) rules.

Rule #2: We Have the Ability to Choose Our Models

This is the heart of flexibility.

You don't have to *believe* X—it's your choice.

It doesn't matter who the hell tells you otherwise or how forcefully they assert it.

It's your life. You have the choice.

I don't care who's championing the model—your parents, your teachers, your priest, or your politician.

They are just as fallible as you are.

Note: It also doesn't mean that everything they say is wrong or not useful. Sometimes it is. Sometimes it isn't. It also doesn't mean they don't have your best interests at heart. Sometimes they do. Sometimes they don't.

Not only do you have the ability to choose what to believe, or to construct varying models of the world, but you can pull yourself in and out of these models at will depending on what suits you.

You have other forms of useful choice control as well.

> You don't have to *focus* on the unhappy X; you can focus on the happy Y.
>
> You also don't have to let those who attempt to influence you have control.

It gets better.

To a certain extent we're even finding that you have a great deal of control over how you *feel* as well.

> You can do physical things to yourself to change how you feel right now:
>
> - Make decisions that improve your health.
> - Choose not to worry (I hereby give you permission).

- Partake in physical actions that bring about a physiological response of happiness (try jumping up and down and *acting* like you're ecstatically happy—how do you feel?—you may be surprised).
- Choose not to let things make you unhappy (I told you I granted you permission).

Rule #3: These Models Can Be Used as Tools (Either for or Against You)

Since your model determines your behavior, it is possible to choose models that serve your interests.

You might want to adopt the belief that you are very attractive. This belief could instill a sense of confidence in you and may have some utility.

Just remember that others can have a certain amount of control over your model, which can be exploited to serve their purposes as well.

The consensus model of entire nations have been deliberately adjusted in order to garner support for wars.

Yes, it's *that* powerful.

For example . . .

Being American I'm tempted to argue for the utility of this poster in rallying support for the war effort. But it's sure interesting to note that the "Murdering Japs" are now some of our closest allies. Notice how the model has changed to suit our purposes at a given time.

The poster is criticizing the International Atomic Energy Agency for being a lapdog of U.S. policy. I must admit, after having spied on the North Koreans for many years while serving in U.S. Army Intelligence, I'm quite reluctant to agree to any propaganda coming out of North Korea. Everything I've seen indicates that they are in fact oppressing and starving their people for the sole purpose of keeping the existing regime in power. But the reality model owned by most North Koreans is wildly divergent from mine. Even the recipients of such oppression are subject to such grandiose model manipulations that they may readily accept harsh treatment as necessary. If you lived in an information vacuum like North Korea and thought your country, no matter how oppressive, was the last bastion of goodness in the world, you'd likely be willing to suffer a great deal for the sake of preserving this "goodness." This "oppression" would even be interpreted as "kindness." Orwell would be proud.

Chapter 5: Rules for UMF

But of course most governments have become far more sophisticated in their attempts to control people. Perhaps the most prevalent method of mass model-control is that of limiting access to information.

This practice, too, can take on very subtle forms.

A great analysis of the more subtle methods can be found in the film *Peace, Propaganda, and the Promised Land.*

You can (and most definitely should) watch the whole thing online here: http://www.informationclearinghouse.info/article 14055.htm

Book III: Disposable Reality

You may (or may not) agree with the political leanings or conclusions of this film, but for the brilliant analysis of the various methods of information control, I feel this film simply must not be ignored. Try to keep your partisanship at bay while viewing and focus on how it brilliantly makes plane the subtle tactics of modern propaganda.

Rule #4: Utility Is the Measure of a Tool's Value

How "useful" is a model? This depends on your aims.

Like a scientific hypothesis, you can test different models of the world as well and see how they suit you.

The key is in understanding that it's a temporary adoption of a model and not a rigid unchanging thing.

Over time, even if it served you in the past, a model can stop serving you, or you can find better ones.

Modeling

In the world of popular self-help manuals there is even the concept of modeling—the practice of deliberately "modeling" someone else's behavior.

That's a whole different thing and it has its uses, but is also dangerous. Rather than looking at someone's abstract model in the scientific sense, the manuals are talking about mimicking someone else's behavior to bring about the same result.

(Continued)

Studying the actions of a pro-football player and modeling what he does, or even what he thinks, as he does it, can bring about miraculous results. It shortcuts the learning curve by totally bypassing any analysis of "why" something works. It can be a truly powerful tool.

But it's hit or miss. You can never know which parts of the person's behavior are bringing about a particular result—so you can't be sure about what to model exactly.

The person you're modeling might be able to paint a picture for you of what's happening in their mind, but of course this may not be an accurate one—and it may not be a picture of what's important.

Modeling, in that sense, is going on every day whether we like it or not.

Sometimes we look at people we admire, and we, usually unconsciously, start picking up their patterns of behavior (remember obedience to authority?).

Sometimes this is good, sometimes not so good.

A kid admires a sports star and then "models" their drug abuse and disrespectful attitude (Yes, to any celebrities or authority figures reading this, "You *do* have a responsibility, and that's why").

Therefore, the problem with modeling as a formal practice is that you can never really know what behaviors or beliefs are bringing about your desired results. (This doesn't mean you should reject the practice entirely, of course. Just be flexible.)

Rule #5: Utility Is Not the Same Thing as Truth

Dave believes he's handsome. In truth, he's actually "one ugly dude."

But believing that he's handsome has served him well as it has made him more confident around the ladies.

But wait a minute: Who says he's "ugly?"

Maybe in 2005 according to a survey conducted by Dave's best friend, 97 percent of the people who look at Dave have a reaction of "ugly dude" when they see him. (For future reference you might want to ask some questions about that survey before blindly accepting the oh-so-authoritative-sounding conclusions. Statistics are commonly misunderstood and distorted.)

Is Dave ugly?

As we read in Book II, information can be twisted, distorted, manipulated, and misunderstood.

Is it possible to ever get down to an "objective reality?"

Who knows?

It may not even exist in the manner you might think.

Because of this uncertainty, there is an opening in your mind that can be exploited. If you adopt the belief that you are good-looking, even if most of the world things you're not, it may have some utility in that it gives you confidence.

It's a hypothesis to be tested, but the difference is enormous: We're not testing in this case whether it's true. We're testing whether believing so serves our purposes.

It should be noted that I'm not advocating just believing any old lie to suit your purposes. I'm also certainly not a proponent of deliberately disseminating or believing disinformation.

From my experience, both disinformation and self-deception are, as a general rule, unhealthy for society and for the mind. More often than not, they will generate undesirable results.

Building a (healthier) model based on what you observe to be true is the better way.

The problem with deliberate deception (either of yourself or of others) is that evidence to the contrary tends to surface. That evidence to the contrary creates dissonance with your model and causes it to dysfunction.

Utility may not equal truth, but the utility of a deception can be severely hampered by contrary evidence.

Rule #6: No Model Is Absolute

As we have seen through history, our global models of the world have changed over time and will likely continue to do so (unless we obtain some form of ultimate omniscience— or, god forbid, ultimately effective mass mind control).

No Model Is Absolute?

If no model is absolute, what about UMF? Yep, that, too.

It is altogether possible that I am completely and utterly wrong about all of this.

After all, throughout this book I demonstrate some very clear bias on a few issues and even some unadulterated hypocrisy (I don't even follow all of Keyes's tools on these pages—shame on me). What the bleep do I know?

Maybe someday we will discover an absolute set of rules that describe the universe clearly, definitely, and irrefutably. If that's the case, flexibility would then work to your detriment. Would it not?

However, despite what many demagogues will tell you, it would seem we have not yet discovered such rules.

Hey, what if one of these guys I brand as "demagogues" is indeed right? What then?

Well, if you focus on utility you won't ever go wrong. That is, if the demagogues' rigid laws of the universe are indeed true and infallible, they will always be useful.

Further, a possessor of such knowledge should encourage questioning. The more you question, the more you should discover they are right.

Right?

So, question away. If they get defensive, angry, or belittle you, it's a possible sign they, too, are not so certain of which they speak.

Rule #7: No Two People Share the Same Model

No matter how similar we are to someone else there will always be differences, and even *minor* differences can greatly affect how we perceive the world.

We may make the assumption that when we've communicated a model to someone that they understand it perfectly.

Without exception, their interpretation of that model is going to vary, at least slightly, from yours.

Rule #8: Models Are Not Mutually Exclusive

One extremely valuable benefit of UMF is the recognition that someone else's model doesn't have to negate yours. Further, you can learn many various, seemingly contradictory, models and apply them as needed.

Most people, when learning a newer model that they think negates a past one, will throw away competing past models entirely.

I hereby give you official permission to stop doing that.

Rule #9: Models Do Not Have to be Accepted in Whole

When a model is *presented* as a complete system, it sets up the presupposition in our mind that it must be accepted as such.

We can, in fact, accept and use (cherry-pick) parts of any given model as suits us.

Including the one outlined in Book IV . . .

Book III: Disposable Reality

Book I:
The Asylum

Why you're stuck where you are now.

Book II:
The Invisible Walls

Your defective mental hardware and other programming anomalies that prevent you from getting what you want.

Offensive weapons used against you to keep you there.

Book III:
Disposable Reality

A new Operating System for the brain.

Defensive weapons to break your way out.

Book IV:
simple•ology
The Simple Science of Getting What You Want

The Programming Language for writing programs that turn dreams into reality.

How to get to where you want to be.

You are here.

*simple•*ology:
The Simple Science of Getting What You Want

Introduction

You may be reading this thinking . . .

Hey, isn't this supposed to be the *simple* science of getting what you want? My head is spinning and none of that was simple.

You're right. What we've been doing is helping you to understand and deconstruct an old dysfunctional, ineffective, complex model and to replace it with a new one that is simple, elegant, and effective.

While the *theory* of *simple•*ology may not be simple, the *practice* of it is. That's the whole point.

You will have experienced this already if you have started using your free companion WebCockpit software and the Daily Target Praxis exercise.

How does it work?

First, let's recap:

Inside our head somewhere is a dream or a vision of something we want to be.

We could follow the straight line path to getting these things, but we don't. Something confuses us along the way.

You may have said to yourself when you were young . . .

I want to be a rock star

. . . and 1,000 voices told you how stupid you were for wanting this—sending your life on their *better* way.

Before we know it, we've become someone we never wanted to become, and what we had wanted is lost.

How did this happen?

Much of the time this is caused by things that we can't see or don't understand: The Invisible Walls.

Book II showed you how to see and then tear down these Invisible Walls.

That is, you learned how to deconstruct the crazy model of the world that comes about from defects and limitations in your brain *hardware*.

Book III showed you how to reconstruct Disposable Walls at will in order to serve your purposes. This is, you create the ultimate Brain OS that allows you to switch models of reality at will in order to serve you best.

Paying respect to the defects and limitations of our brain hardware, UMF provides a foundation for the best way to use it.

But in addition to hardware and an OS, a computer needs programming as well.

Without it, the computer serves no purpose.

You could have the fastest supercomputer in the world and infinite OS flexibility, but if you just flip the switch and let it sit there, what's the use?

When we turn on our computers, we do so with a purpose and to serve those purposes, we need a program.

Some are more efficient than others.

Some, while efficient, are the wrong tools for the job.

How do you know which is which?

Well, a major part of the answer is simplicity.

- Simplicity in purpose.
- Simplicity in method.
- Simplicity in execution.

That's what the practical side of *simple•*ology is all about.

Let's take the computer metaphor to its zenith.

In computer programming, one of the things that separates a good programmer from a great one is what is known as "leanness."

That is, when a computer programmer sets out to write a program, there is an infinite number of ways he can do it. There are infinite variations of the ways he can organize his lines of code to serve a particular purpose.

Bad programs are written like Rube Goldberg machines.

You have probably downloaded computer software in the past that made your computer run slowly or even at times malfunction. This usually happens as a result of excess complexity.

An inexperienced programmer may write 100 lines of code to do the same thing that an expert could accomplish in one.

The leanness of a program allows you to do whatever you're setting out to do in the fastest possible way with the least amount of *stress* on your hardware.

Given that hardware resources are always limited, good lean code is indispensable.

Lean code is often referred to as "elegant", that is, there is something starkly beautiful about a simple, yet astonishingly effective line of code.

In fact, most astonishingly effective things *are* simple.

There is also something elegant and beautiful about living in simple effectiveness as well.

See, the programs we use to get the things we want in our daily lives are usually just as unnecessarily complex. Instead of a straight line path, we take convoluted paths that sometimes lead to nowhere.

Now, some programming languages are better suited for leanness than others. This is why PHP has largely replaced Perl as the most popular programming language for Web applications.

It is possible to do the same thing in PHP with a few lines of code that would take many in Perl.

The 5 Laws of *simple•*ology form the foundation of a new programming language for your brain that will allow you to write lean elegant programs for getting the things you want.

If you've been using your *simple•*ology 101 multimedia companion course and the free WebCockpit software, you'll see that we've provided a programming platform for the language.

The Daily Target Praxis is an exercise you use every day, which allows you to essentially "program" your day using this efficient language.

The power of *simple•*ology comes not only from the leanness of this new language, but from simplicity in purpose as well.

Sometimes we want too many things and the leanest code in the world can't help us. In fact, from my personal experience this is one of the primary failings of otherwise creative and talented people. Instead of focusing on . . .

A limited number of small manageable things

. . . they focus on . . .

An infinite number of unrealistic, unmanageable things

To see what this does to your brain, you can do this with your computer:

1. Open up 20 browser windows.

2. Open up a word processor.

3. Open up a spread sheet.

4. Open up your favorite video file.

Now, if your computer can even function with all of those windows open, try doing all of these things at once:

1. Check stock quotes for 20 different stocks.

2. Compile the current prices of these favorite stocks in a spreadsheet.

3. Write in your word processor a diary entry about what you want most out of your life.

4. Watch your video file.

Well, you don't even have to try this exercise to discover that it can't be done all at once. You'd have to switch back and forth between different windows.

Try it if you don't believe me, but I imagine intuitively you already know what will happen.

One interesting thing to note is that the act of switching between one task and another eats up time in itself. It always takes us some time to *re*focus on a new thing.

Whenever you're interrupted in the middle of a task, you don't just lose the time of the interruption itself but the time it takes you to refocus as well.

Simplicity of purpose shortcuts all of that.

Instead of doing several things at once, you're doing one thing at a time, leveraging the full power of your brain at once.

The WebCockpit software not only helps you to write lean mental programming, but forces you to use simplicity of purpose as well.

Let's learn the basic fundamental rules of this programming language.

This will be, by far, the easiest section of this book to understand and the simplest.

You might have expected that.

Honesty Check

When you read the following chapter, be sure to keep the "rules" of UMF in mind. While the following principles are presented as Laws they are certainly not intended as irrefutable "laws of the universe." (And, no, they weren't passed on to me by an ancient being with a vastly superior intellect whom I channel on Sundays to amuse my friends. Like everything else you read in any other book, these words were written by a guy who may or may not have something useful for you.)

These are merely the laws of "the programming language that is *simple•ology*"—and *simple•ology* is merely a model, the utility of which you can discover for yourself. A programming language is, by definition, a rigid thing. If you write a computer program in Java and don't abide by the rules of Java, it just won't work. While you may, of course, take bits and pieces of *simple•ology* at will to suit your purposes, it is presented as a discrete language for a purpose. My experience (and that of thousands upon thousands who program their minds with this exact language habitually every day) shows that using all of the rules together (and everything else you learn in *simple•ology* 101) as a gestalt will get you the best results. Will you get the same results? Let's try it honestly and find out.

If you discover its utility—great!

If not, we're still friends. I promise.

The First Law of *simple•*ology:
The Law of Straight Lines

The Law of Straight Lines dictates: "The shortest path between two points is a straight line."

You have probably heard this law before, it's one of the basic principles of geometry.

It's pretty simple, really.

If you want to go to New York City from Chicago, you take
the simplest, most direct route. You don't go there via
Siberia.

Similarly, if you want to get a particular result, you don't add
any extra steps. You take the simplest and most direct route.

If you don't understand this law immediately on intuition,
you can experience it practically right now with the following experiment.

This may seem a little ridiculous to you at first, but just bear with me. There's a reason for this that will make perfect sense to you shortly.

Let's begin.

> For this experiment you will need:
>> A glass of water.
>> A timer, watch, or stopwatch.
>
> *Your target:* Take a sip of water. It's a simple target, but it illustrates a profoundly important point.

Here we go.

Place that glass of water on the table in front of you.

Now, take out your timer to see which of the following two methods gets you the desired target in the less amount of time.

> *Method #1: Voodoo*
>
> Start the timer.
>
> Now look at the glass of water in front of you and keep your attention fixed on it.
>
> Close your eyes and say a little prayer for the water. Say, "I ask the universal God-force-in-the-sky to manifest this water in my mouth."
>
> Sit there for a moment and hope that the universe/God/whatever you believe in will bring the water to you.
>
> Take a note of the result.

216

Now, yell at the water. Say, "Hey! You stupid glass of water! Get in my belly!"

Wait for a moment and see if it complies.

Now try sweet-talking the water. Say, "Hey you sexy drink of water you. Why don't you come on up here to my mouth and let me drink ya."

Wait for a moment and see if the water ends up in your mouth.

Next, tell the water, "I just spent $10,000 on a coaching program that is supposed to make me a millionaire in the next year."

See if you have impressed the water enough to make it jump into your mouth.

Finally, look at the water and think some positive thoughts. Smile at it and feel really confident that the water will wind up in your mouth some day if you think positively about it.

Now stop your stopwatch and take note of the time. Also take note of the end result.

Method #2: The Straight Line

Start your timer.

Pick up the water and take a sip.

Set the glass down.

Now stop your stopwatch and take note of the time. Also take note of the result.

Note the difference in time between the two exercises.

217

Also note that at the end of Method #1 you didn't have any water in your mouth.

Here's another way to experience the law.

> Go out to a city block with a friend.
>
> Both of you have the aim of getting across the street. Tell your friend to walk around the block first.
>
> Then you walk straight there.

You don't even have to do this to know what the expected result will be, but it might be useful to do it anyway.

That's the simple and obvious power of straight lines.

Anything you want in life is subject to this same law. Find the fastest and most direct route and the object of your desire is yours.

This seems pretty obvious, right?

But as you know by now, our actual behavior is quite to the contrary. Instead, we get distracted by ourselves or the aims of others.

The Second Law of *simple•*ology: The Law of Clear Vision

The Law of Clear Vision states that in order to hit a target, you need to *see* it clearly.

Imagine an archer shooting at 20 targets. The archer closes their eyes and lets their arrows fly. What's going to happen? Well, they may hit any one of those 20 targets—or they may hit none of them at all.

Hey, what's the problem here? What's so bad about hitting any one of the targets?

The problem is that life isn't always so forgiving.

If this archer were in a contest to see who could hit the middle of target #16, the odds are pretty slim that they're going to win.

Here's another way of looking at it.

If your goal is to get a new car, and you don't see clearly in your mind what kind of car you want, you could just as easily end up with a Ford Focus as a Lamborghini.

In fact, you'd be much more likely to get the Ford Focus because there are so many more of *those* "targets" out there than the nice sports car you want.

Here's a little experiment that will allow you to experience The Law of Clear Vision for yourself.

Let's see which of the following two methods is more likely to get you to your target.

Method #1: Eyes Wide Shut

Note: Please do not do this in a room with any sharp objects.

Stand in the middle of a room with a decent amount of open space and pick out an object on one of the walls. This is your target.

Now, close your eyes and spin around in place. After spinning around at least five times, stop in the direction you think your target is and, keeping your eyes closed, walk toward it.

How close did you get to your target?

Method #2: Clear Vision

Now, stand in the middle of the same room and pick out the same target.

Spin around in place this time with your eyes open and then stop, facing your target and walk toward it.

How close did you get to your target this time?

Repeat both methods as many times as you like.

It's obvious that Method #2 will get you to your target 100 percent of the time. Method #1, on the other hand, will get you there only rarely.

But the real power of clear vision is what you did *before* you started spinning around and walking.

Notice that before anything else *you selected a target!*

Most people go through their lives with targets half-selected or with no target selected at all. What do you think they will achieve?

In order to get what you want, you must have a clear vision of exactly what you want.

The problem is, most of us can't seem to get a clear vision at all. (Your WebCockpit software and companion course will show you how.)

The Third Law of *simple•*ology:
The Law of Focused Attention

The Law of Focused Attention states that in order to hit a target, you must focus sufficient attention on it until you hit it.

If a surgeon were going to give you a heart transplant, do you think he could accomplish this while watching a ball game on television at the same time? You could certainly accomplish eating a bowl of popcorn while watching a game, but I don't think you could pull off the heart transplant.

The things we really want in life sometimes require a lot more attention than we are willing to give.

Let's experience this law firsthand.

Read the following passage and as you do, pay very close attention and try to count how many times I say the word "*simple•*ology."

There once was a time when the people of the village were sad. No matter what they tried, they were never able to get the things they really wanted. Then one day they learned the secrets of simple•ology and the sale of Prozac and Zoloft came to a standstill.

Now, without going back, without peeking, answer the following question:

How many times did I use a word that started with the letter *T*?

You'll notice that you have absolutely no idea how many times I used a word that started with the letter *T*. You may have a guess, but chances are it's not correct.

Your attention was focused on something else. If your attention had been focused on the correct target and if you had exercised focused attention long enough, you would have had no trouble coming up with a fairly accurate answer.

Throughout our lives, most of our attention is focused on things other than our desired targets; this is one of the primary reasons we fail.

Sometimes we focus on what we *don't* want.

Sometimes we focus on the *wrong* target.

Sometimes we focus on simple diversions like television and mindless entertainment.

We may even have a clear vision of what we want, but if we don't have focused attention, we will never hit our targets.

Focused attention by itself is not enough, either. Let's take a look at the next law.

The Fourth Law of *simple•*ology: The Law of Focused Energy

The Law of Focused Energy states that in order to accomplish something you must focus sufficient energy on it until you have done so.

Do you know the difference between a knife and a blunt rock? Most will simply say, "Well, the knife is sharp and the rock is not." That's absolutely right, but what makes a knife sharp?

What exactly is the essence of sharpness?

Quite simply, something is sharp because it has "focused energy."

The point of a knife allows you to focus the energy of your arm movements on a much smaller surface so that you are able to accomplish much more than you could by expending the same energy using a blunt instrument.

Just as a knife can cut more easily the sharper it is, energy becomes more and more powerful the more you focus it.

Let's experience this firsthand ourselves.

Exercise

Note: If you are a child, go find a grown-up before you try this exercise.

Go to your kitchen and get the following items:

A sharp knife.

A spoon.

A cardboard box (a cereal box will do).

Pick up the cardboard box and try to stab it with your spoon. Note how much energy you have to expend before you can pierce it. If you can't pierce the box, that's okay; just move on.

Now, pick up the cardboard box and try to pierce it with your knife. Note much energy it takes to pierce the box.

What you just experienced was concentrated energy.

The surface of the spoon is diffused. When you stab something with it, your energy spreads out among many points.

The knife, however, is focused. A lesser amount of energy will produce a much greater result.

The beauty of it is, you can apply this same principle to almost anything else. It works the same way with your own personal mental and physical energy as well.

(There's more about this "energy" in your companion course.)

The Fifth Law of *simple•*ology: The Inescapability of Action/Reaction

The Inescapability of Action/Reaction states that there are two things from which you can never escape: action and reaction.

In other words, you are *always* acting—even if you think you are not.

> Trying to decide what to do? You're performing the action of deciding.
>
> Thinking about how bad your life is? You're performing the action of thinking about how bad your life is.
>
> Sitting on your butt? Yep, that's an action, too.

The corollary is that for every action we take, there is *some* reaction.

Even if you are just sitting on your butt watching TV, there is a massive symphony of reaction taking place in your body and mind. Your mind is being programmed by what you see on the TV screen. Your body is storing the excess of energy of the food you ate today because you are not burning it off. The forces of gravity are weighing down on your body.

All of that is a reaction to an action you took. We could easily write an entire book on the inevitable reaction to that seemingly simple action.

Here's another way of looking at it.

Did you know that there is really no such thing as procrastination or laziness? These two words presuppose inaction on the part of a person, but such a state does not exist. The word "procrastination" creates a dysfunctional and faulty model of the world.

Why? It's based on an incorrect presupposition (that inaction is possible). You are *always* doing something. "Procrastination" and "laziness" are really just ineffective actions masquerading as *in*action.

So, in order to get whatever you want, all you have to do is stop performing the actions that don't bring about your desired result and start performing the actions that do.

Your WebCockpit software shows you how to do just that.

So, what will *you* do right now?

Given that you have infinite choice, what will you do?

Infinite choice . . .

Wow.

I don't know about you, but I get chills up my spine every time I think about that.

Infinite choice means infinite possibility.

Among those infinite possibilities, I bet there are at least a few that get your heart racing, things in your heart for which you've always thirsted, but that the Invisible (now visible) Walls kept out of your reach.

Are they:

> A superhot dream lover who thinks you are the greatest person who ever lived?
>
> A harmonious family in a loving dream home?
>
> A peaceful place from which you can peer down at the world and revel in its glorious wonders?

Dare you think it?

Do it!

Do it now.

Never stop.

Addendum: The Maintenance Plan for Your New Brain

The moment you put down this book, other models for your life will immediately be competing for control of your brain.

In order to combat this and keep your newer, more useful, Operating System and programming installed, we provide a few simple steps.

Step 1: The WebCockpit

If you haven't done so already, please log in and begin using the WebCockpit software immediately:

http://www.FreeWebCockpit.com.

You'll also have instant access to a number of other cool *simple•*ology tools including the *simple•*ology 101 companion course.

It's important that you do this immediately—*right now*—before you close this book. If you put it off, it's probable you'll get distracted and this opportunity will be lost forever.

Step 2: Creating Your Network

There is one unfortunate result of reading this book: You now have a different way of looking at the world, and the behavior of those around you who don't have these tools may frustrate you.

Not everyone is ready for these ideas, but your life will sure be a lot easier if those around you can communicate in this same way.

Further, there are probably like-minded people within your potential circle of influence who can help you in unimaginable ways.

The following process will allow you to tap into the power of both of these things simultaneously. Here's how.

Simple follow these instructions.

If you are the purchaser of this book, please fill in your name and e-mail address here:

Network Leader

_____
(name)

_____
(e-mail address)

Then, select one person from your life who you think is likely to benefit from these ideas and play along with the rest of this process.

If you are the recipient of this book, fill in this information:

Friend #1

_____
(name)

_____
(e-mail address)

. . . and then e-mail the Network Leader to let them know that you plan to give the book to:

Friend #2

_____
(name)

_____
(e-mail address)

Friend #2: Read the book, fill in the above information, and then e-mail the Network Leader to let them know that the book is about to travel to:

Friend #3

_____
(name)

_____
(e-mail address)

Friend #3: Read the book, fill in the above information, and then e-mail the Network Leader to let them know that the book is about to travel to:

Friend #4

_____
(name)

_____
(e-mail address)

Addendum: The Maintenance Plan for Your New Brain

Friend #4: Read the book, fill in the preceding information, and then e-mails the Network Leader to let them know that the book is about to travel to:

Friend #5

_____

(name)

_____

(e-mail address)

Friend #5: Read the book, fill in the above information, and then e-mails the Network Leader to find out how to return the book to them.

Network Leader: You should be willing to pay the postage. Book postage rates are cheap, so don't worry (or be surprised) if you have to pay to have it sent from across the globe.

You now have a powerful network of people who can think in this flexible and infinite way.

Index